AN INQUIRY
INTO THE
CURRENCY PRINCIPLE

LSE Scarce Tracts in Economics

XI

THE LONDON SCHOOL OF ECONOMICS
SCARCE TRACTS IN ECONOMICS SERIES

AN INQUIRY
INTO THE
CURRENCY PRINCIPLE

Thomas Tooke

Routledge
Taylor & Francis Group

LONDON AND NEW YORK

Published 1996 by Routledge
2 Park Square, Milton Park, Abingdon, Oxon,
OX14 4RN
52 Vanderbilt Avenue, New York, NY 10017

First edition of 1844

First issued in paperback 2018

*Routledge is an imprint of the Taylor & Francis
Group, an informa business*

British Library Cataloguing-in-Publication Data
A CIP record of this work is available from the British Library

ISBN 13: 978-1-138-86549-5 (pbk)
ISBN 13: 978-0-415-14395-0 (hbk)

AN

INQUIRY

INTO THE

CURRENCY PRINCIPLE;

THE

CONNECTION OF THE CURRENCY WITH PRICES,

AND THE

EXPEDIENCY OF A SEPARATION OF ISSUE FROM BANKING.

BY

THOMAS TOOKE, ESQ. F.R.S.

SECOND EDITION.

LONDON:

PRINTED FOR

LONGMAN, BROWN, GREEN, AND LONGMANS,

PATERNOSTER-ROW.

1844.

ADVERTISEMENT

TO

THE SECOND EDITION.

THERE are very few corrections or alterations in the body of the pamphlet. What remarks have occurred on the measures relative to banking proposed by government, and now under consideration, will be found in a Supplementary Chapter.

London, 15th May, 1844.

PREFACE

THE FIRST EDITION.

SOME part of the following pages was written immediately after the appearance of the reports of the
committee of the House of Commons on Banks of
Issue, and the greater part has since been put together
without any definite view to publication.   The reason
which has determined me in now publishing them is,
that whether the views here presented be assented
to or not, they are such, I think, as ought not to
be wholly overlooked in the consideration of the
measures which the government has announced its
intention of proposing to Parliament in the course
of the present session, with a view to placing the
banking system of the United Kingdom on an improved and permanent footing.

Some of the points which I have endeavoured to
establish may probably be thought not to be made
out with sufficient fulness of explanation, and doubtless on several of the topics a more exhaustive
process of proof and illustration might be required
for the purpose of anticipating and answering ob-
jections.   But such a process could not be comprised
within a readable compass.   It would require a book
instead of a pamphlet.

The necessity for compression, which I feel to be thus imposed upon me, has prevented me from touching at all upon topics which are of importance and connected in some points of view with the subject here discussed, but to which justice could not be done in an incidental notice.

One of the great difficulties of dealing with the subject about to be discussed, as indeed in most cases of controversy, but in this more than in most others, arises from the use of the same words in different senses, that is, from a shifting of the meaning of the term, when applied indiscriminately in the same argument to designate things and processes totally distinct: not to mention the mooted points, as to whether deposits, bankers' cheques, and bills of exchange should be considered as money or currency; because these involve rather definition and classification, according to the purposes for which they are supposed to be employed, than that loose and ambiguous use of terms to which I allude.

It will be seen in the course of this discussion how much of the obscurity and perplexity and error, in which the objects of inquiry are involved, may be traced to the vague and ambiguous language commonly employed in treating of them : such for instance as "gold and silver," "the precious metals," and "bullion," used indiscriminately and synonymously with "money" and "currency;" the terms "money and currency" employed when "capital" is meant. "Issues of paper," meaning bank notes, for mere advances of capital where no bank notes pass; — the "value of money or currency," for the rate of interest or discount. "Abundance and cheapness, or scarcity and dearness of money," to signify a lower or a higher rate of interest, or a tendency to either. And " expansion and contraction of the currency, or of the circulation," when undue extension of credit, and its consequent revulsion, would be the correct description of the facts of the case.

The instances in which confusion and inconsistency in reasoning may be traced to this loose and ambiguous use of language are innumerable ; and if I could hope that by directing attention to the sources of error so pointed out, and thus induce more care and distinctness of phraseology, so as to render future discussions on the subject more intelligible, and consequently to narrow the grounds for difference of opinion, I should consider that my labour in this publication has not been thrown away, even although I should fail of gaining assent to the conclusions, or any part of them, which I have endeavoured to establish.

London, March, 1844.

ERRATUM.

Page 159. line 17. from the bottom, for " management" read " direction."

AN INQUIRY

THE CURRENCY PRINCIPLE,

ETC. ETC.

INTRODUCTION.

IT was held by most writers of any authority on the subject of the Currency, till within the last few years, that the purposes of a mixed circulation of coin and paper were sufficiently answered, as long as the coin was perfect, and the paper constantly convertible into coin; and that the only evils to be guarded against by regulation, were those attending suspension of payment and insolvency of the banks, a large proportion of which blend an issue of promissory notes with their other business. This, in point of fact, is what is understood in general terms as the banking principle, and is that upon which our system of currency is constructed and conducted.

But a new canon of currency has of late been promulgated by persons of no mean authority. According to these authorities, it is not sufficient that the bank notes should be at all times strictly convertible into coin, and that the banks, whether issuing or not issuing, should be solvent; they consider that a purely metallic circulation (excepting only as regards

B

the convenience and economy of paper), is the type of a perfect currency, and contend that the only sound principle of a mixed currency is that by which the bank notes in circulation should be made to conform to the gold, into which they are convertible, not only in value, but in amount; that is to say, that the bank notes being supposed to be a substitute, and the only substitute, for so much coin, should vary exactly in amount as the coin would have done if the Currency had been purely metallic; and that the test of good or bad management is not, as is considered under the mere banking principle, in the extent or proportion of reserve in treasure and in immediately convertible securities held by the banks; but in the degree of correspondence between variations in the amount of bullion, and variations in the amount of bank notes in circulation. A regulation of the issue of bank notes, in conformity with this doctrine, is now understood to be designated as the Currency principle.

With a view to the application of this principle to practice, it has been suggested that either a national bank should be established under commissioners, whose duty and functions should be confined to the exchange of paper against gold, and of gold against paper, for all beyond a fixed amount of paper issued against securities; or that the Bank of England should be the sole source of issue, under the strictest rule of separation of the functions of issue from the merely banking department.

The arguments urged in favour of such separation have, as it should seem, made considerable impression on the public mind, and schemes founded upon this principle have been strongly pressed on the attention of government, on the ground not only of guarding against the danger of suspension and insolvencies, but of imparting more confidence and stability to credit and trade, and of securing greater steadiness in prices, and thus obviating or abating the alternations of feverish excitement, and the extreme of depression, which have prevailed under the existing system, and which are imputed to a neglect of the Currency principle.

The question whether the constant convertibility of the paper can, or cannot, be preserved and maintained under a prudent management, on the existing footing of a union of issue and banking, will be considered hereafter. But, waiving for the present all consideration of the question of security against suspension and insolvencies, it is desirable to examine the grounds on which it is contended that other evils, besides the danger of non-convertibility and insolvencies of banks of issue, arise out of the present system as compared with the currency-principle system, and that the test of good or bad management of the country banks of issue consists, not in the amount of their reserves in gold and available securities, compared with their liabilities, but in the conformity of the variations of their circulation to those of the circulation of the Bank of England; while the test of the management of the Bank of England is in the conformity of the variations in the amount of its circulation to those of the efflux or influx of the precious metals.

CHAPTER I.

STATEMENT OF THE CURRENCY PRINCIPLE.

THE theory of the Currency principle numbers among its advocates many distinguished names. The fullest and most elaborate statements of it, however, are to be found in the publications of Mr. Norman, Mr. Loyd, and Colonel Torrens, and in the evidence of the two former gentlemen before the Committee of the House of Commons on Banks of Issue in 1840. I therefore avail myself mainly of their exposition of the doctrine, and their arguments in support of it, as affording the best grounds for an examination of the theory, and of the practice recommended as an application of it.

The following extract from Mr. Norman's evidence conveys a concise statement of the theory, and of the proposed application of it, as the only sound rule for the paper portion of the currency, namely bank notes, which he limits to those notes which are in the hands of the public : —

" I consider a metallic currency to be the most perfect currency, except so far as respects inconvenience in some respects, and cost. In every thing else a metallic currency is the most perfect, and should be looked upon as the type of all other currencies ; and as from their superior convenience and greater cheapness, bank notes are introduced to supply the place of a certain portion of metallic currency, I think that bank notes should be so managed, that they should possess all the other attributes of a metallic currency, and among those attributes, I conceive the most important to be that they should increase and decrease in the same way that a metallic currency would increase and decrease. I do not think it is possible to improve upon a metallic currency, except in the two points of convenience and cheapness." *

Mr. Norman afterwards explained, that by convenience he meant the easier transfer, and by cheapness, the economy of using the less costly material; so that the paper, thus regulated, would be so far an improvement on a metallic currency.

The following are the chief † evils which present themselves, according to Mr. Norman's view, in our existing paper circulation, from its not conforming to such rule: —

1. A tendency to vary, both as to excess and deficiency, in an unnecessary degree, and at unsuitable periods.

2. A liability to discredit, both mercantile and political, in a large portion of it, if not the whole.

3. Temporary or permanent insolvency on the part of many of the issuers.

Mr. Loyd in his evidence gives the following view of the inconvenience, which he ascribes to the present system : —

Q. 2748. "Are there any other evils besides the danger of nonconvertibility that arise out of the present system?" A. "There can be no doubt about it; the state of the circulation has a very direct effect upon the state of credit, of confidence, of prices, and of banking; and if the state of the circulation be allowed to become an unnatural one, unnatural and pernicious effects will be produced upon all those. If your circulation is subject either to depreciation from excess of its amount, or to violent fluctuations of amount, then undoubtedly that will be followed by corresponding effects upon confidence, upon credit, upon prices, upon banking, and so forth. Those things are also affected

* G. W. Norman. Evidence. Committee on Banks of Issue. Question No. 1749.

† "Remarks on Currency and Banking," by G. W. Norman, 1838.

by other considerations. I do not see that it is possible to analyse the effects, and to attribute to each cause its respective share in producing those effects; all that can certainly be understood is, that if you regulate the paper circulation upon sound principles, you may be quite sure that you have then removed that portion of the evil effects which was attributable to the want of due regulation."

By an unnatural state of the circulation, and the want of due regulation, must be understood, in the sense in which Mr. Loyd uses the term, a non-conformity of the amount of bank notes to the amount of bullion.

CHAP. II.

MODE OF OPERATION OF A METALLIC CIRCULATION.

ADMITTING, for the sake of argument, that a metallic circulation is the type of a perfect currency, it should seem that those who confidently pronounce it to be so, labour under a most egregious misconception of what the working of it would be.

Upon the grounds which I have now to state, it will be evident that the operation of a perfectly metallic circulation would not be attended with the advantages which they contemplate; nor, on the other hand, with the disadvantages which might be apprehended, if it were to work as they seem to imagine it would.

According to the Currency principle, every export of the precious metals under a metallic circulation, would be attended with a contraction of the amount and value of the currency, causing a fall of prices, until the degree of contraction and consequent fall of prices should be such, as by inducing a diminished import and increased export of commodities, to cause a reflux of the metals and a restoration of prices to their proper level. So, on the other hand, an influx of the precious metals would raise prices, till they reached a level at which the converse of the process would take place. This oscillating process of a rise and fall of prices with every influx or efflux of the precious metals, independently of circumstances connected with the cost of production of commodities, and the ordinary rate of consumption, would be perplexing enough, and any thing but convenient to the commercial, or the manufacturing, or the agricultural community.

The advocates, however, of the doctrine contend that, although thus the oscillations might be more frequent, the scale of them would be more contracted, every divergence being more quickly checked. I firmly believe, however, that if every export and import of the precious metals were attended with the effects imputed to them by this theory, the inconvenience would be felt to be intolerable; and that some of what Mr. Norman calls economising expedients would be devised and applied as a remedy.

But the operation would not be that which the theory, as it is stated in the following passages, supposes: —

"It is universally admitted by persons acquainted with monetary science, that paper money should be so regulated as to keep the medium of exchange, of which it may form a part, in the same state, with respect to amount and to value, in which the medium of exchange would exist, were the circulating portion of it purely metallic. Now, it is self-evident, that if the circulation were purely metallic, an adverse exchange, causing an exportation of the metals to any given amount, would occasion a contraction of the circulating currency to the same amount; and that a favourable exchange, causing an importation of the metals to a given amount, would cause an expansion of the circulating currency to the same amount. If the currency of the metropolis consisted of gold, an adverse exchange, causing an exportation of gold to the amount of 1,000,000*l.*, would withdraw from circulation one million of sovereigns."— TORRENS. *Letter to Lord Melbourne, pp.* **29, 30.**

" The amount of the import or export of the precious metals, is a pretty sure measure of what would have been the increase or decrease of the amount of a metallic currency."— S. J. LOYD. *Further Reflections on the Currency, page* **34.**

And Mr. Norman, after explaining the manner in which the exchanges, as between two countries, A and B, may be rendered adverse to A, so as to cause an export of coin or bullion, goes on to say—

" The export of coin and bullion will cause general prices to fall in country A, and to rise in B, supposing the debt to B not to be sooner discharged, until it becomes more advantageous to export goods than money."—*Letter to C. Wood, Esq. M. P., p.* 17.

In these passages, and many more that might be cited, it is assumed that the precious metals, gold, and silver, and bullion, are synonymous with currency and money, and are convertible terms. And accordingly every export of the precious metals is not only considered, in the supposition of a metallic circulation, as a contraction of the currency of this country; but as so much added to the currency of the country to which it is exported. Such alteration in the relative quantity of the metals in the respective countries from which or to which they are transmitted being, according to this theory, an abstraction or addition of so much money ; and prices, that is, the general prices of commodities, being considered as depending on the quantity of money, a corresponding rise or fall of them is assumed to be the consequence. In this view some very important considerations are overlooked.

Before entering upon them, however, I must premise, that throughout this discussion the value of gold in the commercial world is assumed to be constant, *i. e.* that the cost of production and the general demand are unvaried; also that the tariffs of foreign countries are *in statu quo*, so as to confine the consideration to the effects of an influx or efflux of bullion on the currencies of the respective countries, divested of any reference to disturbing causes, beyond those incidental to the course of trade and international banking.

There is, and must generally be, in a country like this or like France, a stock greater or less of gold and silver, beyond that which is in use as money or as plate, or which is in the mint, and in goldsmiths' and silversmiths' hands, in preparation for use as either. This surplus or floating stock may be considered as seeking a market, whether for internal purposes or for export; and, be the quantity greater or less, can it be said of it, if it is exported, that the amount is so much abstracted from the currency of the country, any more than if an equal value of tin or zinc, or lead or iron were exported?

Moreover, of that part of the stock existing in the shape of coin in this country it may be observed, that as the coinage is not subject to a seignorage, there may be, and frequently is, in that shape a considerable amount of the precious metals which may not be in the hands of the public, circulating as money, nor in the reserves of the different banks, the Bank of England excepted; but may, like the uncoined metals, be seeking a market at home or abroad. It may be in the coffers of the Bank of England; but held as bullion, being in the shape of coin equally convenient for every purpose, and more convenient for some purposes, in that form, besides that of serving for currency, than in uncoined gold, that is, in bars or ingots.

The idea of gold seeking a market, and not immediately finding one, may seem strange, and by the firm believers in the currency-principle doctrine may be set down as paradoxical and absurd.

Gold is an object in such universal demand, or in other words so universally marketable, that its being supposed to be kept on hand at all, under the uncertainty of finding a suitable market for it, appears to be inconceivable, or almost a contradiction in terms.

I am ready to admit that gold is a commodity in such general demand that it may always command a market, that it can always buy all other commodities; whereas, other commodities cannot always buy gold. The markets of the world are open to it as merchandise at less sacrifice upon an emergency, than would attend an export of any other article, which might in quantity or kind be beyond the usual demand in the country to which it is sent. So far there can be, I presume, no difference of opinion.

But there will be found to be no inconsiderable difference, if we distinguish as we ought to do, for the purpose whether of theory or practice, between gold considered as merchandise, *i. e.* as capital, and gold considered as currency circulating in the shape of coin among the public.

Mr. Senior, in one of his lectures on the value of money, observes, " The value of the precious metals as money must depend ultimately on their value as materials of jewellery and plate; since if they were not used as commodities, they could not circulate as money." And he makes a remark to the same effect in an article in the " Edinburgh Review" for July last, on Free trade and Retaliation. " The primary cause of the utility of gold is of course its use as the material of plate. The secondary cause is its use as money." Of the truth of these propositions there can be no doubt.

In a new and enlarged edition, just published, of that vast repertory of various and important information, " The Commercial Dictionary," Mr. M'Culloch, after weighing different authorities, gives the following estimate of the consumption of the precious metals for purposes distinct from their use as money:—

" According to this view of the matter, the present annual consumption in the arts will be — the United Kingdom 2,500,000*l.*; France, 1,000,000*l.*; Switzerland, 450,000*l.*; the rest of Europe, 1,600,000*l.*; in all, 5,550,000*l.* To which adding 500,000*l.* for the consumption of North America, the total consumption will be 6,050,000*l.*

" But a portion of the gold and silver annually made use of in the arts, is derived from the fusion of old plate, the burning of lace, picture frames, &c.

" Assuming that, as a medium, twenty per cent., or one-fifth part, of the precious metals annually made use of in the arts, is obtained from the fusion of old plate, we shall have, by deducting this proportion from the 6,050,000*l.* applied to the arts in Europe and America, 4,840,000*l.* as the total annual appropriation of the new gold and silver dug from the mines to such purposes, leaving about 4,400,000*l.* a year to be manufactured into coin, and exported to India," &c.

Mr. M'Culloch estimates the present annual produce of the precious metals from the American, European, and Russo-Asiatic mines, at 9,250,000*l.**

* Although the question of the total annual produce of gold and silver may not be considered as having any immediate bearing on the point now under discussion, it is a matter of such general interest, especially as relates to the vast increase of gold in Siberia and the Oural district of Russia, that I am induced to give Mr. M'Culloch's view of the quantities produced from the several sources which he specifies. After stating from the most recent authorities the quantities produced from the South American and Mexican mines, he goes on to observe with reference to the produce of the Russian mines —

" In addition to the quantity of 631 poods obtained from washings in Siberia in 1842, the silver obtained from the mines of Kolyvan yielded, in the course of the same year, 30 poods of gold, while the

As this country is not only a large consumer of the precious metals for purposes other than money, but is also an entrepôt for receiving from the mines,

washings and mines of the Oural mountains yielded no fewer than 310 poods; making the total produce 971 poods; equal to 35,030 lb. avoirdupois, or 42,571 lb. Troy, which, at 46*l.* 14*s.* 6*d.* per lb. is equivalent to 1,989,128*l.* 11*s.* — (*Supplement au Journal de l'Intérieur* for 1842, p. 16.)

It is necessary, however, to bear in mind that the Russian government imposes a duty, varying, according to circumstances, from 20 to 25 per cent., on the produce of the mines and washings; and there can be no doubt that the temptation to avoid so heavy a duty, and the peculation on the part of the agents for the Crown, must give rise to a great deal of smuggling. Perhaps, under such circumstances, we should not be far wrong if we estimated the metal of which no account is taken at $\frac{1}{4}$th part of the above; but taking it only at $\frac{1}{6}$th part, we have a sum of no less than 2,386,000*l.* for the produce of the Russian gold mines and washings in 1842.

It may be supposed, perhaps, that it would be wrong to take the produce of the Russian washings and mines in 1842 as a fair criterion of their future produce, seeing that the produce of the washings in that year was not far from being twice as great as it had been in any previous year. But it is to be observed, that the produce in question has been progressively and rapidly augmenting during the 13 years ending with 1842; and it is stated in the official journal whence we have borrowed these details, that *selon toute probabilité, et à moins qu'on ne manque d'ouvriers, le chiffre de l'année* 1843 *offrira de nouveau sur celui de l'année dernière un excédant très-considérable.*[1]

" In addition to this vast quantity of gold, Russia produces a quantity of silver, which may, perhaps, be estimated, at an average, at about 1,300 poods a year, worth, at 5*s.* 2*d.* an ounce, 193,440*l.*

" We have seen no very recent accounts of the produce of the Saxon, Hungarian, and other European mines, on which it would be at all safe to place much reliance. We incline, however, to think that their produce may be safely estimated at about 750,000*l.* a year.

" Hence, supposing we are nearly right in these estimates, the total available produce of the American, European, and Russo-Asiatic mines will be, S. American and Mexican, 5,600,000*l.*; U. States, 100,000*l.*; European, 750,000*l.*; Russo-Asiatic, 2,600,000*l.*; making in all, 9,050,000*l.* And therefore, should these estimates be not very wide of the mark, it may be concluded, in opposition to the commonly received opinions on the subject, that the supply of the precious metals is at present but little inferior to what it amounted to when the American mines were most productive.

[1] We have since learned, as this article was going to press, that the produce of the Russian gold mines and washings in 1843 amounted to no less than 1342 poods! being equivalent, adding one fifth for the quantity not brought to account, to 3,298,962*l.* 11*s.* 1*d.* sterling; an increase which is altogether extraordinary, and will have the most powerful influence.

and distributing the greater portion of the quantity
applicable to the consumption of other countries, the
bullion trade, totally independently of supplying the
currency, must of necessity be very considerable.
In resorting to this entrepôt the metals can only be
considered as merchandise in transit, seeking a market
for consumption either in this country or abroad.
But beyond the stock which is requisite for this
purpose, and which must always include more or less
of surplus to meet occasional extra demand, there
must be a very considerable amount of the precious
metals applicable and applied as the most convenient mode of adjustment of international balances,
being a commodity more generally in demand, and
less liable to fluctuations in market value than any
other. I will not venture, in the absence of any re-
cognised grounds for computation, to hazard an estimate of the amount so required; but bearing in mind
the immense extent of international transactions ; and
the vicissitudes of the seasons, and other circumstances affecting the relative imports and exports of
food, and raw materials, and manufactures, besides
the variations in the market value of national and
private securities interchangeable, it cannot but be
that the quantity of bullion required to be constantly
available for the purpose must be very large ; the
principal deposits of it being in the Bank of England,
the Bank of France, and the public banks of Hamburg and Amsterdam. These deposits may, moreover, in some of the public banks, be swelled by coins
which have become superfluous in the circulation.

If, therefore, we take into account the magnitude
of the stock necessarily imported, partly for the consumption of plate in this country, and partly for that
abroad, and of the amount required as available funds
for the adjustment of international balances, it may
not be deemed an extravagant supposition that there

might occasionally be under a perfectly metallic circulation fluctuations, within moderately short periods,
to the extent of at least five or six millions sterling
in the import and export of bullion, perfectly ex-
trinsic of the amount or value of the coin circulating
as money in the hands of the public, and perfectly
without influence on the general prices of commodities, as equally without general prices having been a
cause of such fluctuations.

It may be objected that the quantity of bullion
which I have supposed to be in deposit among the
principal public banks of the commercial world, applicable to the adjustment of international balances,
should be looked upon as performing the functions of
money, in restoring the level of the currencies, which
the very fact of the necessity for the transmission of
money from one country to another proves to have
been disturbed. This objection is founded on the assumption that gold and silver are money or currency,
and it is supposed that the transmissions of bullion
for the purposes in question have a direct operation
upon the amount of money or currency in actual circulation in the several countries. But in this objection
the consideration is overlooked, that the coins only
which enter into, that is, form part of the internal
circulation of the country, can be designated as currency, while bullion can only be viewed in the light
of capital.*

---

* With the exception of Mexican dollars, this being the form in
which the produce of the silver mines of America is mainly distributed,
and Imperials, the golden coin of Russia, being the form in which the
extraordinarily large and increasing produce of the Asiatic provinces of
that empire is adding to the general supply of the precious metals ; and
further excepting the gold coins of this country, which, being issued
without any charge whatever for manufacture, are found to be for some
purposes of export more convenient than bars or ingots : with these exceptions, the instances are rare in which, unless depreciated at home by
compulsory paper money, the coins usually circulating as money are
withdrawn to supply foreign payments of any magnitude.

The distinction between bullion, as merchandise or capital, and coins, as money or currency, may be exemplified in the case of coins which are subject to a seignorage, and in cases such as that of Hamburg, where the money current for all the ordinary expenditure of income consists chiefly of a variety of foreign coins, passing from hand to hand at a conventional value, while all mercantile payments are made by transfers of capital, deposited in the form of fine silver, and called bank-money.

In such a case as that of Hamburg there have been, and must often again be, very great fluctuations in the amount of silver in the bank, and consequently of bank money, without any obviously corresponding variations in the amount of money in circulation for current purposes of expenditure by the community, or any variation as arising from that cause in the general prices of their commodities. And if a seignorage were imposed on the gold coin of this country on correct principles (that is, accompanied by a limitation of tender, and by a power on the part of the holders to demand gold bullion at 3l. 17s. 10$\frac{1}{2}d$. per ounce), there might be, and there would be, supposing a purely metallic circulation, occasionally very considerable variation in the amount of bullion in the coffers of the national bank, or in the hands of dealers in bullion, without necessarily in the slightest degree affecting the amount of the currency actually in circulation, in the ordinary daily transactions arising out of the expenditure of individuals composing the public, and without variation in general prices.

The views, of which an outline has here been sketched, distinguishing bullion as a commodity, constituting the readiest means of international transfers of capital, from the currency employed for internal purposes, will be rendered more clear when I come to point out, as I shall presently endeavour to do, an important distinction between that part of the circulating medium which is employed in the transfer and distribution of capital, from that which is employed in the expenditure of incomes, that is, in the retail trade of the country. And I do not now enter more fully into detail as to what I conceive would be the working of a purely metallic circulation, because that question does not form the main ground of the present inquiry, which is as to the sufficiency of the arguments adduced in accordance with the theory of the currency principle, in favour of an entire separation of the functions of banks of issue from those of ordinary banking.

In the doctrine which it is my purpose here to examine, the perfection of a metallic circulation is assumed to be beyond question; while the imperfection of our present system of paper credit, quite apart from the danger of inconvertibility, is pointed out and enlarged upon, by reference to the degree in which it is asserted to depart from this assumed model of perfection, — a model of whose properties and mode of operation the most erroneous notions seem to be entertained by those who set it up.*

* In the text I have taken what may be called the mercantile view of the question of international temporary movements of the precious metals, the general value of them being assumed to be constant; and this view I am persuaded is the correct one, for the purpose either of practical application, or of intelligible explanation of the actual course of commercial affairs. As to the more general and abstruse question of the laws which determine the more permanent distribution of those metals among the nations of the earth, constituting the level of the currencies of different countries, as exhibited in their general prices, and in wages especially, valued in gold and silver, it would require, in order to have justice done to it, a more scientific exposition, embracing a much wider range of reasoning and of facts than would comport with the scope or purpose of my present argument.

CHAP. III.

MISTAKEN VIEW BY THE CURRENCY THEORY OF THE WORKING OF THE EXISTING SYSTEM.

IF sufficient grounds have here been adduced to give rise to, at least, a suspicion that the propounders of the currency theory are unaware, or rather are under a total misconception, of what would be the working of a purely metallic circulation, we are inevitably led to suspect, or rather I should say to conclude, that they may and do labour under a misconception fully as great, not only as to what would be the working of a mixed circulation of coin and bank notes, administered according to the currency principle (that is, so as to conform to what they suppose would be the working of a metallic circulation), but as to what the working of it actually has been and is under the existing banking system.

The misconception which, as it should seem, they labour under, may be referred mainly to the view which they take of bank notes, as being essentially distinct in all their attributes and functions from each and every other of the component parts of the circulating medium, and as coming exclusively along with coin under the designation of *money*.

Bank notes, accordingly, they call *paper money*, and ascribing, as they do, a direct influence to the quantity of money on the state of trade, of confidence, and credit, and on prices, they attach great importance to the fact of any increase or diminution of bank notes in circulation, more especially as regards a conformity, or non-conformity, of such increase or diminution to variations in the amount of bullion. As

C

therefore they conceive that it is in the power of the banks of issue so to regulate the amount of their notes in circulation, as to conform to variations in the amount of bullion, or, as it is more commonly termed, to regulate their issues, by the exchanges (inasmuch as attention to the exchanges will serve to indicate whether gold is coming in or going out, or likely to come in or go out), they consider the conformity or discrepancy between the fluctuations in the amount of bank notes in circulation and the amount of bullion in the coffers of the Bank of England, as the test or criterion of the good or bad management of the banks.

On occasions of marked discrepancy, the persons who espouse the currency principle, and are, at the same time, favourable to the Bank of England, charge the country banks with counteracting, by their inattention to the exchanges in regulating their issues, all attempts of the Bank of England to restrain the general circulation within due bounds; while the country banks, both private and joint-stock, maintain, through their organs, that it is not in their power to determine what shall be the amount of their notes in the hands of the public. And not content with thus repelling the charge made upon them, they retort it upon the Bank of England, which, according to them, has the control of the whole circulation, and expands or contracts the amount according as suits its own purpose.

It appears to me that neither of these parties is right in charging the other; and, moreover, that those persons who, on the part of the public, judging only by the criterion set up by the currency theory, namely, by the conformity of variations in the amount of bank notes to variations in the amount of bullion, charge the present system with causing irregularity in the circulation, and with all the evils which flow from bad regulation, are equally far from a right judgment.

I am quite convinced, and will endeavour to show, that the amount of bank notes in circulation, that is, out of the walls of the issuing banks, and in the hands of the public, furnishes no criterion of good or bad management by the banks of issue, and is not an efficient cause operating upon trade and confidence and credit, and upon prices; and that, excepting the greater inconvenience attending the insolvency of an issuing than of a non-issuing bank, there is no difference between the two descriptions of banks as regards their influence on the value of the currency.

I cannot help thinking that there is a lurking impression among the doctrinaires of the currency theory, arising mainly from their use of the term "issue of paper money," which leads them to confound bank notes strictly convertible into coin, with a compulsory and inconvertible paper currency. It is true, no doubt, that they are aware that the liability to payment on demand in gold will eventually check any excess of issue in the one, and will thus distinguish it from the other. But it seems to me equally true, judging by all their expressions and the whole course of their arguments, that they are misled by a false analogy, and that although they admit in general terms that there must be a check to the power of issue by its being brought to the test of convertibility, they are of opinion that there is a power in each individual bank of issue, and in the banks of issue collectively, to operate at any given time in adding directly to the amount of bank notes in circulation, and in withdrawing them from it. The presumption that the advocates of the currency principle are under the influence of this mistaken analogy will be strengthened when we come to the consideration of the effects on trade, credit, and prices, which they ascribe to the influence of the quantity of money, meaning bank notes and coin. In the mean time it may be proper to bestow some remarks on the reasoning by which it is' proposed to be proved that bank notes differ in all essential properties, as regards the performance of the functions of money, from all other forms of paper credit employed in the business of interchange.

CHAP. IV.

DISTINCTIVE PROPERTIES ASCRIBED TO BANK NOTES.

MR. NORMAN, after noticing what he calls the contrivances usually resorted to for the purpose of either dispensing with the use of money altogether, or of diminishing the quantity of it, which is absolutely required for the adjustment of existing transactions, observes, —

" On these contrivances one general remark may be made, as it affords a ready and practical, if not a strictly scientific distinction between such substitutes for money, and that which, as I conceive, really constitutes money, viz. coin and bank notes. If bank notes are withdrawn from circulation, their place must necessarily be supplied by an equal amount of coin; but the abolition of any, or of all of the contrivances for dispensing with the use of money, will not necessitate the introduction in their place of an equal amount of coin or bank notes."—*Letter to C. Wood, Esq., p.* 34.

In dealing with this proposition, let us try it by putting the case in the strongest way, and suppose that the Bank of England has the power, and is disposed to withdraw all its notes from circulation ; or, in order to obviate the objection, that in such case other banks might supply the vacuum, let us suppose that all promissory notes, payable on demand, were suppressed by act of parliament. Would Mr. Norman contend, that the whole amount must of necessity be replaced by coin? Most assuredly such would not be the effect.

A moment's consideration must be sufficient to satisfy any one that it would only be the smaller denomination of notes, which, if suppressed, would require to be replaced by coin ; the whole of the 1*l.* notes which still circulate in Ireland and Scotland, would require to be so replaced, and the greater part of the 5*l.* notes, and a small part of the 10*l.* notes, in the United Kingdom.

All the larger amounts might be, and most probably would be, supplied by cheques and bills of exchange and settlements.

The employment of the higher denominations of Bank of England notes is chiefly for the following purposes : —

1. Collection of the public revenue, and the payment of it into the Exchequer.

2. Payments on sales and mortgages of landed and other fixed property. Till lately the rule in transactions of this nature, was almost uniformly that the payment, on conveyance of the deeds, should be made in bank notes. But there has of late been a tendency to relax this rule, and cheques are now not unfrequently received in payment on such occasions.

3. Dividends and rents received by persons who do not employ bankers.

4. Payments for debts in cases in which the debtor has not a banker, or in which he would not be trusted so far as to have his cheque received in satisfaction of the claim.

5. Payments into Court in litigated claims.

6. Reserves held by bankers, and especially those

of the west end of the town, and by the joint-stock banks in the city who are not admitted to the clearing-house.

7. Settlements at the clearing-house.

Now these are peculiar purposes, most or all of which might be answered by other means than bank notes, and most assuredly not by supplying their place by coin.

1. The public revenue is, in an increasing number of instances, paid into the Exchequer by drafts on the Bank of England.

2. Payments for landed and fixed property are in an increasing number of instances paid by cheques.

3. Dividends to persons not keeping bankers, might be retained by them in the shape of warrants.

4. and 5. Involve so small an amount, as not materially to affect the question.

6. The circulation of Bank of England notes among bankers, whether between the Bank of England and the west-end bankers, and the city joint stock bankers, and the circulation of country bank notes, in settlements among each other, are mere conventional transfers of capital, which, with

7. The clearings among the bankers of the city of London, might all be effected either by Exchequer bills, as in the case of the banks of Edinburgh, or by cheques on the Bank of England.

The country bank notes above the lowest denominations, (which are in use in the retail trade, and in the payment of wages,) are mostly employed in the provision markets, and in cattle and horse fairs, purposes for which, as I shall proceed to show, bills of exchange were formerly, and might be again very extensively employed.

CHAP. V.

DEPOSITS AND CHEQUES.

AMONG the contrivances which the currency theory allows to be the means of dispensing with the use of money, although it will not admit that they perfectly perform the functions of money, are deposits or lodgements in banks, subject to certain stipulations of repayment. In the examination by the Committees on Banks of Issue in 1840, there seems to have been a great waste of time and temper in the discussion of the question, whether deposits should be considered as currency, and as performing the functions of money.

There is an obvious objection to speaking of deposits in general terms as performing the functions of money, inasmuch as deposits are of different descriptions as to the conditions of repayment attaching to them. But supposing the deposits to be strictly payable on demand, there is still an apparent impropriety in ascribing to them quâ deposits a direct agency or activity.

It sounds oddly, to say the least of it, to speak of deposits or lodgements of money as being active. The activity, if any, is in the payment by cheques founded upon the deposits. It is not the deposits, but the transfers of them; or, in other words, the cheques, that constitute the actual instruments of interchange, and effect payments concurrently with bank notes. They perform the functions of money not only as perfectly as bank notes, but in the description of transactions to which they are applicable, they are more convenient than bank notes.

They obviate the trouble of paying fractional parts of the sum in coin; they, in many cases, supersede

c 4

the use of stamped receipts, inasmuch as the books of
the bankers serve as evidence of the payment. They
obviate the risk of robbery or fire, which attends the
possession of bank notes by persons not having the
accommodation of strong and fire-proof safes. The
cheque books of the drawers serve also to preserve a
counterpart of all the particulars of the payment, and
so assist in tracing error or irregularity, if there be
any, in the payment or in the entry of it. And the
use of crossed cheques, as far as regards the London
bankers who resort to the clearing-house, admits of
the drawers of such cheques adjusting their receipts
and payments between the opening of business and
half-past three or four o'clock, so as that their banker
shall have only the balance to pay, or receive, or set
off. Some or all of these advantages, with possibly
others, which may exist and may have escaped my
observation, are sufficient to account for the great
and increasing tendency to the employment of cheques
in preference to bank notes in the pecuniary transactions of the metropolis and of the metropolitan
district.* Independently of the greater convenience
which is found to attach to the use of cheques instead
of bank notes, by persons who are in the habit of
employing bankers, the employment of bankers by
persons, whether traders or not, of the middle classes
(the upper classes of course, all, or nearly all, employ
bankers), is daily gaining ground, and this is an additional cause of the displacement of bank notes by
cheques.

There is every reason to believe that a much larger

* In illustration of the tendency to a preference of the use of cheques
over bank notes in mercantile transactions in London, it may here be
observed, that if a merchant in the course of his business receives
Bank of England notes of 100*l.* or upwards, and has on the same day to
pay away a sum or sums exactly equal to the notes, he will in most
cases make his payment by a cheque or cheques, and put the bank
notes into his banker's, to be placed to his credit against his drafts.

amount of payments in the metropolitan districts is effected by drafts on bankers than by bank notes. And the circumstance that deposits payable on demand are the foundations on which drafts are passed, such drafts effecting more payments than bank notes, seems to be the ground on which the late Mr. Page in his evidence (and Mr. Hume in his examinations, his views being identical with those of Mr. Page) contended that deposits are currency and more active in making payments than bank notes.

Qu. 770. (Mr. Hume.) " As you have stated that circulation and deposits are both currency, which of the two do you consider to be most active in making payments?"

An. " Deposits beyond all question."

I do not, as I have before had occasion to observe, concur in the propriety of applying the term currency to deposits, because, although such of them as are payable on demand may and do serve for payments by the means of transfer, it is the transfers or cheques, and not the deposits, which, in point of fact, constitute the instruments of exchange. But whether deposits payable on demand, or only the drafts against them, are to be considered as currency, is immaterial to this part of my argument, which is to show that, as instruments of exchange, cheques, or the deposits on which these are founded, answer the purposes of money, as conveniently in nearly all instances as bank notes, and more conveniently in most cases *; and that therefore whatever influence may be ascribed to bank notes, whether on prices, or on the rate of interest, or on the state of trade, cannot be denied to cheques or to their substratum, deposits payable on demand.

* There is a great saving of coin in paying by drafts instead of bank notes. In payments by bank notes all fractional parts of *5l.* must be paid by coin. Upon the very numerous payments in the Kingdom (Ireland and Scotland, where *1l.* notes still circulate, excepted) the saving of coin thus effected must amount to a considerable sum.

CHAP. VI.

BILLS OF EXCHANGE.

THAT transactions to a very large amount are adjusted by bills of exchange has long been known and admitted in general terms; but the vastness of the amount was not brought distinctly under the notice of the public till the appearance of a pamphlet by the late Mr. Leatham, an eminent banker at Wakefield. According to a computation, which he seems to have made with great care, founded upon official returns of bill stamps issued, the following are the results: —

RETURN OF BILL STAMPS, FOR 1832 TO 1839 INCLUSIVE.

	Bills created in Great Britain and Ireland, founded on returns of Bill Stamps issued from the Stamp Office.	Average amount in circulation, at one time in each year.
	£	£
1832	356,153,409	89,038,352
1833	383,659,585	95,914,896
1834	379,155,052	94,788,763
1835	405,403,051	101,350,762
1836	485,943,473	121,485,868
1837	455,084,445	113,771,111
1838	465,504,041	116,376,010
1839	528,493,842	132,123,460

Mr. Leatham gives the process by which, upon the data furnished by the returns of stamps, he arrives at these results; and I am disposed to think that they are as near an approximation to the truth as the nature of the materials admits of arriving at. And some corroboration of the vastness of the amounts is afforded by a reference to the adjustments at the clearing house in London, which in the year 1839 amounted to 954,401,600*l.*, making an average amount of payments of upwards of 3,000,000*l.* of bills of exchange and cheques daily effected through the medium of little more than 200,000*l.* of bank notes. As illustrative of the position for which Mr. Leatham contends, and conclusively, as I think, that bills of exchange perform the functions of money, he observes, —

"For a great number of years, it had been the custom of merchants to pay the clothiers in small bills of 10*l.*, 15*l.*, 20*l.*, and so up to 100*l.*, drawn at two months after date on London bankers. I have always considered this the best part of our paper currency, ranking next to gold ; the bills existing only for limited periods, and acquiring increased security as they pass from hand to hand by endorsement. From the unreasonably high stamp laid on small bills in 1815, the merchants have ceased to pay in bills, but pay notes instead, requiring 2*d.* in the pound for cash from the receiver ; and I find the revenue has much decreased in consequence in this class of stamps."—pp. 44, 45.

Mr. Lewis Loyd, when examined by the House of Lords' Committee on the Resumption of Cash Payments in 1819, gave the following evidence :—

Qu. 9. At the time when you began business in Manchester, in 1792, were there any country banks which issued notes in that town, or in any other part of Lancashire ?

An. None, I believe.

10. Have there never been, at any time, country banks issuing notes in Lancashire ?

None within my recollection. I began to reside in Manchester in 1789. There had been, before that period, notes issued there about the year 1787 or 1788 ; I think by a bank which failed. I believe that was the only attempt ever made in Lancashire till lately, except that there was lately, and is now, an attempt made to issue them at Blackburn.

11. How has the circulation of Lancashire been carried on since the period to which you refer ?

Wholly in Bank of England notes and bills of exchange.

12. Is the proportion of Bank of England notes very considerable as compared with bills of exchange?

About one-tenth, I think, in Bank of England notes, and nine-tenths, at least, in bills of exchange. These bills of exchange circulate from hand to hand, till they are covered with endorsements.

13. Is any inconvenience felt from this mode of circulation by bills of exchange?

None whatever.

14. Has the circulation of Bank of England notes increased or decreased of late years in proportion to bills of exchange?

I think the proportion of bank notes has increased.

15. To what do you attribute that increase?

Partly to the great increase of the stamp duties. It is within my knowledge, from the transactions of my own house, that the supplies of provisions, which are drawn from the neighbouring counties, used to be paid for in small bills of exchange, mostly of 10*l.* or lower; but now the persons going to the neighbouring localities for supplies of provisions take with them bank notes and bank post bills, stating that the stamp is too serious an object to them to be paid on such small sums. There is scarcely a day when I do not send 2000*l.* in bank post bills for that purpose to Manchester, which we hardly ever used to do before the last addition to the stamp duty.

16. Were these bills of exchange drawn for specific loans previous to their employment, or were they bills resulting from antecedent transactions?

Those who purchased provisions used to go to fairs and markets with bills ready drawn in their favour, very often for specific sums, as for the round sum of 10*l.*, just as they now take 10*l.* in Bank of England notes and bank post bills. There was this peculiar circumstance attending them, that the bills were usually drawn at two months' date, and were considered as cash payment; they were bills drawn on London by country bankers, and remitted to London as suited the convenience of the parties who received them. Now, in consequence of having bank post bills and Bank of England notes, the persons who receive the bills make an allowance to those who pay them of two months' interest.

My answer applies to the supply of the town with provisions. Nearly all the other transactions of Manchester, except the payment of labourers, are still carried on in bills of exchange, and the payment of labourers is mostly made in 1*l.* Bank of England notes.

If by an alteration in an opposite direction, the stamp duty on bills of exchange were reduced or abolished, while that on promissory notes on demand remained the same, and still more, if it were raised, there would be a considerable change in practice, by making the smaller payments among dealers in bills of exchange as a substitute for bank notes.

In a work by the late Mr. Henry Thornton *, which attracted considerable attention at the time, and which formed the subject of an article by Mr. Horner, in the first Number of the Edinburgh Review in 1802, there is a distinct and full description of the manner in which bills of exchange performed in his time the function of money; a description which is strictly applicable at the present day. He observes with reference to bills of exchange, —

" They not only spare the use of ready money, they also occupy its place in many cases. Let us imagine a farmer in the country to discharge a debt of 10*l.* to his neighbouring grocer, by giving to him a bill for that sum, drawn on his corn-factor in London, for grain sold in the metropolis; and the grocer to transmit the bill, he having previously endorsed it to a neighbouring sugar baker, in the discharge of a like debt, and the sugar baker to send it, when again endorsed, to a West India merchant in an out-port, and the West India merchant to deliver it to his country banker, who also endorses it, and sends it into further circulation. The bill, in this case, will have effected five payments, exactly as if it were a 10*l.* note payable to bearer on demand. It will, however, have circulated in consequence chiefly of the confidence placed by each receiver of it in the last endorser, his own correspondent in trade; whereas the circulation of a bank

* " An Inquiry into the Nature and Effects of the Paper Credit of Great Britain."

note is rather owing to the circumstance of the name of the issuer being so well known as to give to it an universal credit. A multitude of bills pass between trader and trader in the country in the manner which has been described; and they evidently form, in the strictest sense, a part of the circulating medium of the kingdom.

" Bills, since they circulate chiefly among the trading world, come little under the observation of the public. The amount of bills in existence may yet, perhaps, be at all times greater than the amount of all the bank notes of every kind, and of all the circulating guineas. Liverpool and Manchester effect the whole of their larger mercantile payments, not by country bank notes, of which none are issued by the banks of those places, but by bills at one or two months' date, drawn on London. The bills annually drawn by the banks of each of those towns amount to many millions."

The late Sir Francis Baring, writing at a still earlier period (1797), and of a state of things within his immediate experience, refers, in the following passage, to the practice prevalent among country bankers, of issuing notes payable after date or after sight,—

" In the beginning of the year 1793, and of the present year, 1797, the banks of Newcastle stopped payment, while those of Exeter and of the West of England stood their ground. The partners in the banks at Newcastle were far more opulent, but their private fortunes being invested could not be realised in time to answer a run on their banks. Their notes allowed interest to commence some months after date, and were then payable on demand; by which means they had not an hour to prepare for their discharge. The banks of Exeter issued notes payable twenty days after sight with interest, to commence from the date of the note, and to cease on the day of acceptance. There can be no doubt that the practice of the banks at Newcastle is more lucrative, whilst it must for ever be more liable to a return of what has happened. The twenty days received at Exeter furnishes ample time to communicate with London, and receive every degree of assistance which may be required." *

* " Observations on the Bank of England, and on the Paper Circulation of the Country," p. 17.

If, according to the currency theory, the circumstance that written promises to pay being after date or sight, and to order, and therefore requiring an endorsement, are disqualified from being considered as performing the functions of money, on what ground is it that bank post bills, which are after sight and to order, have been always included in the returns of the circulation of the Bank of England? They are by their form strictly bills of exchange, being not only after sight and to order, but commonly used for transmission by post; and if these are considered to be part of the circulation, on what ground are the bills of the Bank of Ireland, and of the chartered Banks of Scotland, and of such banks throughout the United Kingdom as are of undoubted credit, not included in the return of the country circulation? This applies indeed only to short-dated bills of the most unquestioned credit; longer-dated bills, of more doubtful security, seem to have been alone in the view of those persons who assert the exclusive title of bank notes to be considered as money. Bills of this description, that is long-dated bills, are sometimes not used for purposes of circulation,—they are simply written evidence of a debt which is discharged at maturity, without passing into third hands. I will not stop now to enter into the distinction between long and short-dated bills in the comparison with bank notes, and between bills drawn by bankers, and bills by merchants or dealers on dealers. It is a sufficient negative of the main proposition on which the currency theory rests, to have shown that short-dated bills of exchange are substitutes not only for coin, but for bank notes.

If, as a last resort in the argument, it be said that bills of exchange require the intervention of bank notes for the ultimate payment, the answer is, that this is a mere fiction, for that in fact the adjustment takes place by settlement, and that a small amount of bank notes for the balance effects the liquidation, which might equally be effected by drafts on the Bank of England; or, as is done in Scotland, by exchequer bills. An alteration in the stamp duties has, as stated by Mr. Lewis Loyd and Mr. Leatham, operated against the employment of the smaller bills of exchange instead of bank notes. If the case were reversed, the stamps lowered on bills and raised on notes, we should see an immense increase in the former, and a great diminution in the latter, — in other words, bank notes would be withdrawn, and bills of exchange supply their place.

It is hardly perhaps necessary to advert to the latter part of the proposition quoted at page 20., viz., that the abolition of any or of all the contrivances for dispensing with the use of money, will not necessitate the introduction in their place of an equal amount of coin or bank notes. There surely can be little doubt but that the abolition of such contrivances would necessitate the substitution of an equal amount of bank notes or coin.

Sufficient grounds have, as I venture to think, been stated for establishing the claim in behalf of cheques on bankers, and of bills of exchange, to be considered as performing, concurrently with bank notes, the functions of money for the purposes for which they are respectively used.

If the propounders of the currency theory would confine their distinction in favour of bank notes to the lowest denominations, namely, the 1*l.* notes wholly, and the 5*l.* and 10*l.* notes partially, it might, as I have already observed, be conceded; but then what becomes of the dogma or the axiom of Mr. Norman and Mr. Loyd, on which the currency theory is made to rest?—and what becomes of the inferences which they have drawn as to the management of banks, from a view exclusively to the whole of the circulation, large notes as well as small? In truth, their tests of good and bad management, and their views of the purposes and properties of the whole of the circulating medium and of its component parts, are essentially defective and erroneous. They draw distinctions which are not real or substantial, as, for instance, of the higher denomination of bank notes compared with bills of exchange and cheques; while they totally overlook and confound the distinctive character of the instruments of interchange which are used in the distribution and expenditure of incomes, as compared with that of the instruments which are used in the distribution and employment of capital.

CHAP. VII.

DISTINCTION OF CIRCULATION AS BETWEEN DEALER AND DEALER, AND BETWEEN DEALER AND CONSUMER.

IT is of the greatest importance to a clear view of the working of the present system that the distinctive characters of the instruments of interchange should be observed and defined. Dr. Adam Smith has noticed the distinction, and has accordingly, in his views of the operation of paper money, steered clear of the confusion between currency and capital which pervades and disfigures nearly all modern reasonings on the subject.

" The circulation of every country," Dr. Smith observes, " may be considered as divided into two " different branches — the circulation of the dealers " with one another, and the circulation between the " dealers and the consumers. Though the same pieces

" of money, whether paper or metal, may be em-
" ployed, sometimes in the one circulation and some-
" times in the other, yet as both are constantly
" going on at the same time, each requires a certain
" stock of money of one kind or another to carry it
" on. The value of the goods circulated between the
" different dealers with one another never can exceed
" the value of those circulated between the dealers
" and the consumers, whatever is bought by the
" dealers being ultimately destined to be sold to the
" consumers. Paper money may be so regulated as
" either to confine itself very much to the circulation
" between the different dealers, or to extend itself
" likewise to a great part of that between the dealers
" and the consumers. When no bank notes are cir-
" culated under ten pounds value, as in London,
" paper money confines itself very much to the circu-
" lation between the dealers. When a ten pound
" bank note comes into the hands of a consumer he
" is generally obliged to change it at the first shop
" where he has occasion to purchase five shillings'
" worth of goods, so that it often returns into the
" hands of a dealer before the consumer has spent a
" fortieth part of the money." *

There can be no doubt that the distinction here
made is substantially correct. Bearing in mind this
distinction, the reason is obvious why, as far as relates
to the interchange between dealers and consumers
(including the payment of wages, which constitute
the principal means of the consumers), coin, and the
smaller denomination of notes serving as coin, are
essential to such interchange, and why, consequently,
if those smaller notes are withdrawn, their place must
be supplied by coin; but not so as regards the interchange between dealers and dealers. Bank notes are

* " Wealth of Nations," M'Culloch's edition, pp. 141, 142.

not only not essential to that interchange, but it must be manifest to any one having even a slight knowledge only of the manner in which such interchange is conducted, that, in point of fact, bank notes are rarely used in the larger dealings of sales and purchases.

The great bulk of the wholesale trade of the country is carried on and adjusted by settlements or sets-off of debts and credits, the written evidences of which are in bills of exchange (including in that term all promissory notes payable to order after date), while current payments for what are called cash sales are mostly discharged by cheques; the ultimate balance only, arising out of the vast mass of such transactions, requiring liquidation in a comparatively small amount of bank notes. The principal exceptions to this, I apprehend, are in the provision trade, and in the sheep and cattle and horse fairs, in which the payments are mostly made in coin and bank notes; but there can be no question that for amounts of 10*l*. and upwards, bills of exchange might be, as they formerly were, and, but for the increased stamp duty, would be, substituted.

Of the fact that, with the exception of these, and perhaps of some few other wholesale trades in which no credit is given, there is little or no intervention of bank notes in purchases or sales among wholesale dealers, no doubt can be entertained. And I have now to state the explanation, which I am not aware of having met with among the various lucubrations on the subject of the currency which it has been my lot to see, of the reason why, with the exceptions I have pointed out, such sales and purchases are effected without actual payment in money, which, by the currency theory, is defined to be coin or bank notes.

The reason is, that all the transactions between dealers and dealers, by which are to be understood all sales from the producer or importer, through all the stages of intermediate processes of manufacture or otherwise to the retail dealer or the exporting merchant, are resolvable into movements or transfers of capital. Now transfers of capital do not necessarily suppose, nor do actually as a matter of fact entail, in the great majority of transactions, a passing of money, that is, bank notes or coin — I mean bodily, and not by fiction — at the time of transfer. All the movements of capital may be, and the great majority are, effected by the operations of banking and credit without the intervention of actual payment in coin or bank notes, that is, actual, visible, and tangible bank notes, not supposititious bank notes, issued with one hand and received back by the other, or, more properly speaking, entered on one side of the ledger with a counter-entry on the other. And there is the further important consideration, that the total amount of the transactions between dealers and dealers must, in the last resort, be determined and limited by the amount of those between dealers and consumers.

The business of bankers, setting aside the issue of promissory notes on demand, may be divided into two branches, corresponding with the distinction pointed out by Dr. Smith of the transactions between dealers and dealers, and between dealers and consumers. One branch of the banker's business is to collect capital from those who have not immediate employment for it, and to distribute or transfer it to those who have. The other branch is to receive deposits of the incomes of their customers, and to pay out the amount, as it is wanted for expenditure, by the latter in the objects of their consumption. The former may be considered as the business behind the counter, and the latter before or over the counter: the former being a circulation of capital, the latter of currency.

The distinction or separation in reasoning of that

branch of banking which relates to the concentration of capital on the one hand and the distribution of it on the other, from that branch which is employed in administering the circulation for local purposes of the district, is so important in its bearing on the question of regulating the circulation by the foreign exchanges, and on that of the connection between the currency and prices, that the fullest elucidation of the practical operation of that distinction may naturally be required. I have, therefore, as the best method of elucidating this point, drawn largely on the examinations by the Committee on Banks of Issue in 1841; and if it be objected that more than enough of the evidence is here adduced for the purpose, seeing that the point is so clear when simply stated, my answer to the objector is, that simple and clear as the distinction may appear to him, so imbued were the members of the Committee who took a prominent part in the examination, with the tenets of the currency theory, as to have remained apparently (judging at least by the reiteration of their questions to the same effect) unconvinced of the powerlessness of the banks of issue to influence directly the amount of the circulation of Bank notes. And even to this day, with all the light of subsequent experience, it should seem, judging by speeches and publications, and the declamations against excessive paper issues, which still appear occasionally on the subject, that the dogma of the power of banks of issue to create paper money *
ad libitum prevails to nearly as great an extent as ever.

* By *paper money* being always understood, according to the doctrine under consideration, Bank notes in the hands of the public.

D 3

CHAP. VIII.

REGULATION OF THE CIRCULATION BY THE FOREIGN EXCHANGES.

ALL the country bankers examined concur in stating that they have not the power by loans or discounts beyond the ordinary transactions of the neighbourhood to extend or contract the local circulation of notes, or to influence prices. They could, indeed, refuse to issue their own notes in answering the demands of their depositors, but such refusal must be accompanied by offering Bank of England notes or coin, and thus the local circulation would be equally filled up; they may curtail or call in their advances and so diminish their engagements, and eventually render a smaller amount of circulation necessary; but the immediate demands for notes for local purposes must still be satisfied.

It appears by that evidence, that their circulation is devoted and confined to local purposes, chiefly in small amounts, for the retail trade; and in the rural districts, in advances to farmers for the purchase of stock and seed, and to cattle dealers and provision merchants: but that when called upon to make advances by way of loan or discount on a larger scale, it is always by a draft or order upon London, or upon such of their correspondents in other towns as happen to suit the borrowers — such loans or discounts being invariably made out of capital, or, in other words, out of the general resources of the bank.

Among the country bankers of England I have selected the evidence of Mr. Stuckey, the head of the admirably conducted banks of Somersetshire under his firm, because there is no one more conversant, both theoretically and practically, than he is with the subject of banking. By his position formerly he was in intimate communication with Lord Liverpool and Mr. Huskisson. He was examined by the Bullion Committee in 1819. He was an adherent to the principles of the late Mr. Ricardo; and he expressed opinions of the desirableness of having the circulation of bank notes regulated by a view to the foreign exchanges.* But what is the result of his very large experience as a banker?

477. (*Chairman.*) Do you conceive that, generally speaking, there is an insuperable difficulty in country banks exercising such a controul over their own issues, as to reduce them to some extent during a period of adverse foreign exchange? *I really do not see how that is to be done.*

---

* The regulation of issues by the foreign exchanges is an expression which, like all the rest of the language of the currency theory, conveys no clear description of the actual process. One would suppose that the directors of the Bank of England, who profess to regulate their issues by the foreign exchanges, attend to the variations in the quotations, and according as these indicate an adverse or a favourable tendency, regulate their issues, or rather their advances, accordingly. No such thing. It is only by the influx or efflux of bullion that they are guided, and very properly so. It is impossible for any but Exchange-jobbers to judge of the quotations, allowing for agios, and dates, and distances. And the idea that country-bankers could judge of them! The evidence of Mr. Palmer before the Committee on the Bank Charter in 1832, is decisive on this point:—

122. "How do you regulate your issues according to the foreign exchanges? — By the notes being returned for gold or silver for export."

123. "Do you regulate them from the returns you have of what the foreign exchanges are, or from the action which takes place upon the Bank? — The action which takes place upon the Bank."

125. "Do you not sometimes anticipate the actual action upon the Bank, by the demand for gold, when you see there is a tendency in the foreign exchanges to produce that action? — No; we wait for the actual demand."

It is clear that in point of fact the directors are and can be guided only by the state of their treasure; and that, instead of the expression of "regulating the circulation by the foreign exchanges," the terms descriptive of the actual process should be, "regulating the securities by the efflux or influx of bullion."

478. Then what is the practical effect of the regard to foreign exchanges, which you think all country bankers ought to pay?

The practical effect is to make them more cautious and circumspect in the management of their money transactions; but I should not state, that in the agricultural districts, the circulation would be altered by the foreign exchanges.

479. Do you conceive, that although the country bankers ought to pay regard to the state of the foreign exchanges, it is not in their power to bring that regard into practical effect by reducing the amount of their issues during the period of adverse exchange?

I do not see how it could be done.

480. Will then the regard which you recommend they should pay to the foreign exchanges produce any practical effect whatever upon their issues?

Yes, it would produce effect in the management of their monied concerns.

481. What practical effect would it produce on their *issues?*

Very little; my own opinion is, that country issues have very little to do with exchanges.

482. Would the regard which you recommend to the foreign exchanges produce any effect upon their issues?

Very little; it would produce some effect upon the management of their monied concerns.

483. (*Sir T. Fremantle.*) Upon their liabilities?
Yes.

484. *But comparatively little on their issues?*

Yes: particularly in the agricultural parts of the country.

485. Upon what do you think the issues of the country bankers depend?

More on the state of agriculture than any thing else. When the landed interest is in a comfortable state, I consider the issues to be increased.

491. (*Sir T. Fremantle.*) The advance which you make to the agriculturists is an advance of capital, whether it is paid to them in your own notes, or Bank of England notes or gold?

Yes; the advance is generally made to agriculturists in our own notes.

492. But if the state of the country is such as not to require an increase of your own issues, you are quite sure that those notes will come back to you in the course of a short time?

Exactly.

493. Therefore the advance that you make in that case *is an advance of capital, and not an advance of mere issue?*

Exactly; it is made out of our resources.

501. (*Chairman.*) Will you state how you are affected by foreign exchanges?

I think the London banker is affected by them, therefore I am affected; I naturally know that if my deposits are withdrawn, and any demand is made upon me, I must sell my securities; therefore I look to the foreign exchanges in order to ascertain how the money market is, that I may know what securities I shall dispose of.

524. (*Chairman.*) Suppose the case of an adverse foreign exchange, when, according to your own opinion, the paper circulation of the country ought to be reduced, would you, on a depositor asking for the payment of a deposit in notes, be at all guided by the circumstance of the foreign exchanges, as to whether you paid that deposit in Bank of England notes, or in your own local notes?

I admit that I should not be guided by the foreign exchanges, but I should be guided by knowing where the deposit money was to go to.

525. (*Sir T. Fremantle.*) You have stated that when you have observed gold going out of the country, and money becoming tight in London, you have been in the habit of issuing directions to your different branches, to be more circumspect in the advances they make; has the effect of that been practically to diminish the amount of your notes in circulation in those districts?

I do not think it has; I am not aware that it has.

526. What has the effect been?

To make them *more cautious in their advances,* keeping our resources more within our own command; instead of discounting a bill, which we should discount under some circumstances, we have refused it; and instead of advancing

1000*l.* or 2000*l.*, we have desired the person to take 500*l*; therefore we keep our banking capital and banking resources more under our own command.

527. But are you prepared to say that the circulation of your own notes has not been affected by that course of conduct?

I am not aware that it has.

537. Supposing, for instance, it should ultimately be thought that it is desirable that the country circulation should have a general conformity to the state of the foreign exchanges, do you conceive that this could be in any way effected by the country bankers?

I do not at present know how it could be accomplished; and I may take the liberty of going further in that question, and saying that it appears to me that the country issues, as conducted in the west of England, have very little or nothing to do with the foreign exchanges.

538. Do you conceive then that the only circulation which ought to have reference to the foreign exchanges is that of the Bank of England?

I do conceive that it is the only thing which ought to have reference to them, being the circulation of London, and London being the spot where the foreign exchanges are generally effected.

539. (*Mr. Grote.*) Do you mean to state that you think the circulation of the Bank of England ought to be made to vary in conformity with the foreign exchanges, but that the circulation of the country banks ought not to be affected by the foreign exchanges?

No, I do not go so far as that; my opinion is that the country circulation does not affect the foreign exchanges, because it is a different kind of circulation; the foreign exchanges are, we all know, affected in various ways, but I do not think they are affected by the country circulation, and I have looked attentively at that question.

The evidence of Mr. Gilbart, of the London and Westminster Bank, of Mr. Hobhouse, of a bank at Bath, and of Mr. Rodwell, of a bank at Ipswich, is full of information as to the circumstances which influence and limit the country circulation without the possibility of reference to the exchanges. But as these gentlemen do not profess ever to have entertained an opinion of its being desirable, if it were practicable, to regulate the country circulation by the foreign exchanges, I have preferred a reference to Mr. Stuckey's evidence, he having entertained and professed an opinion that it was desirable, but had made the discovery, confirmed by long experience on a very extensive scale, of its utter impracticability.

Mr. Gurney was examined on this point by the Committee on the Bank Charter in 1832. I have before had occasion to notice his evidence at some length*, and will now only refer to the concluding part of it : —

Does it not follow from what you have said, that an over-issue of notes of country bankers cannot easily be effected?

My belief is that it cannot be effected by any act of the country bankers.

As far as this point is concerned, it might perhaps be deemed to be sufficiently proved by the evidence already adduced. But not the evidence only on this point is confirmed, but also much additional light is thrown on the distinction between capital and currency, by a view of the Scotch system of banking. The examinations of some of the managers of the Scotch banks by the Committee in 1841, are accordingly well worthy of attention as illustrative of that distinction.

* "History of Prices," vol. iii. p. 193.

CHAP. IX.

SCOTCH BANKING. REGULATION BY FOREIGN EXCHANGES,
AND DISTINCTION BETWEEN CAPITAL AND CURRENCY.

THE evidence of Mr. Alexander Blair, treasurer and
manager of the Bank of Scotland, which is the oldest
of the chartered banks, having been established in
1695, and which appears to be conducted with great
ability and prudence, is full of valuable information
as to the machinery and working of the Scotch system of banking.

He mentions a curious fact relating to the mode in
which the balances resulting from the exchanges
twice a week among the banks are adjusted by the
means of exchequer bills which, to the amount of
450,000l., they hold for that express purpose. Here
we have exchequer bills answering all the purposes
that Bank of England notes at the clearing house in
London do.

Mr. Blair also states that seven millions in amount
of notes is found to be requisite in order to keep up an
average circulation of three millions,—a very curious
fact, as it appears that the stamp duty is paid upon
the whole stock, whether in the hands of the public
or within the walls of the banks, and that the whole
amount is out in circulation for a few days at two
seasons of the year.

It is stated, moreover, upon the same authority,
that the total amount of deposits which, in 1826, was
computed to be about twenty-one millions, had in
1841 reached to about twenty-seven millions.

It is a remarkable circumstance that, while there
has been a great extension of banking capital, and of
banking accommodation, and of banking competition,

in Scotland since 1826, the amount of the aggregate circulation has considerably diminished. What a commentary upon the received doctrine of the power of banks to increase their issues of paper money as suits their interests or convenience; and that it is the effect of the competition of banks of issue to create a vast mass of worthless paper.

Mr. Blair gave the following statement of the increase of banking accommodation in Scotland: —

"There are about 380 bank offices in Scotland, of which 348 are branches. The population may be stated at 2,500,000; thus there is one bank for every 6600 individuals.

"There were in 1825, 167 offices, of which 133 were branch banks. The population being then 2,200,000, there was one bank to every 13,170 individuals.

"The amount of notes exchanged per annum by the banks of Scotland is believed to be not under 100,000,000l. delivered, and 100,000,000l. received. The Bank of Scotland alone delivers 10,000,000l., and receives in exchange as much."

But the immediate purpose of my reference to the evidence of Mr. Blair and other managers of the Scotch banks, is to show that they do not and cannot regulate their *circulation* by the foreign exchanges; and that, when they make advances, it is out of their capital or that of their depositors, without any direct influence on their circulation; that they attend to the conduct of the Bank of England in regulating their *advances*, which, however, have no immediate influence on their *circulation*.

Mr. Blair was asked by the chairman, —

Do you conceive that the amount of notes in circulation should be regulated in any way with reference to the state of the foreign exchanges? — I conceive that the loans and discounts of banks should be regulated with reference to the state of the foreign exchanges, *but I would not consider it necessary to regulate the circulation by the foreign exchanges.*

1879. (*Mr. Grote.*) Then, is it your opinion that, at the same time when the Bank of England is contracting its circulation, for the purpose of correcting an unfavourable exchange, the provincial banks should proceed in the same track, and contract their circulation also?

I think that they should consider the action of the Bank of England, at that time, with reference to their general rules of discount. *I would beg to leave the circulation out of the question;* I would say that the banks should look to the amount of their loans and discounts under such circumstances; and, at the same time, I would say, that the Bank (of England) should keep a large reserve, to be determined by their past experience and observation, for which, to the extent it is held for public account, they should receive compensation.

1880. Then, is it your opinion, that at a period when the exchanges are unfavourable, and the Bank of England are contracting their circulation, the provincial banks ought to be more cautious in granting loans and discounts than they were before?

Certainly.

1881. (*Sir J. R. Reid.*) Does your bank act upon that principle?

It does.

The examinations, however, of Mr. Kennedy, manager of the Ayrshire Bank, and of Mr. Anderson, of the Glasgow Union Banking Company, went more particularly to the question of the distinction between capital and currency; and their evidence is calculated to throw great light on this point.

Mr. Kennedy is asked:—

2092. (*Mr. Grote.*) You stated that the causes affecting the quantity of your notes which were out in circulation at any time, were, in your opinion, independent of the action of the foreign exchanges?

I did.

2093. But you also stated that at the time when the foreign exchanges were unfavourable, and when there was a pressure upon the money market, you thought it imperative, as a measure of prudence, to realise some of your reserves and to call in funds from Edinburgh or London?

Yes, that is an accurate representation.

2094. Then do you not think that that act of yours, in bringing into your country funds realised in Edinburgh or London is, in point of fact, tantamount to your acquiring for yourself a certain portion of the London currency or the Edinburgh currency, inasmuch as the local increase of your currency is not at that moment tantamount to the increase of the aggregate currency of the country?

But we do not bring into our country the Edinburgh or London money. The diminution of our reserves takes place in this way: parties have payments to make in Edinburgh or London or other places, and we draw upon our reserves there to meet those payments, *but we do not bring down gold or Bank of England* notes from the London market in order to pay them away in our country.

2095. Though you may not actually bring down gold or Bank of England notes, is not the effect of your diminishing the amount of your reserve in Edinburgh and London, and increasing by that means the advances to certain local borrowers, *tantamount to bringing down so much of the Edinburgh or London currency into your locality?*

I cannot see that I bring any currency down; it is merely a payment made in London, or in Edinburgh, from one party to another.

2096. Will you describe in what way your reserves are usually kept?

In easy negociable securities, such as exchequer bills and short-dated bills of exchange, money lying in our banker's hands in London, and in other parties' hands in London, and money lying in our agents' hands in Edinburgh and Glasgow, and other places.

2097. Suppose you sell so many thousand exchequer bills either in London or in Edinburgh, of course the proceeds of those exchequer bills are placed to the credit of your agent, whether your Edinburgh agent or your London agent?

Yes.

2098. In that case, when you direct those funds to be paid out, *you do in point of fact dispose of an equal amount of London currency or of Edinburgh currency for the purposes of your bank?*

Yes.

2099. Then, in point of fact, do you not consider that you are enabled by means of *that portion of the London currency or the Edinburgh currency* of which you thus acquire the disposal, to obtain a certain increase of the amount of notes in your own district, and does not that, in point of fact, occasion a certain *diminution in 'the London or the Edinburgh currency* which may be set against the increase of your own local issues at the time?

But when I give a draft upon the London agent I do not in consequence of the increased sum that I have put at his command give out notes for it. I give a draft upon London payable to some party in London; the money is paid over in London, so that I do not make an issue upon that.

2100. But *the quantity of currency* which is available to other parties in London or Edinburgh is diminished by that portion which you draw for your own use?

I do not see how it diminishes the quantity of currency in London: it merely transfers it from one party to another.

2101. If you were not to employ that portion of *the London currency which you acquire* by realising your exchequer bills, that portion would be at the disposal of some other person in London for the purpose of granting accommodation to London borrowers?

But I do not take it out of London; it is still in the hands of some party in London.

2102. But if by means of that operation you are enabled to extend your accommodation to your local borrowers, you do make it serviceable to the wants of your district, and is it not tantamount, in point of fact, to a transfer of so much capital from employment in London to employment in Ayrshire: is not that the general effect of the operation?

That may be the effect of it; but it has no effect in diminishing the amount of the currency in the London market. I do not bring out of London any currency; I merely take the currency from one party in London, and give it to another.

2103. Do not you bring down from London to Ayrshire a certain portion of capital which was before in London?

I do not see that.

2104. If the effect of this transaction be to enable you to supply the wants of borrowers in Ayrshire, which otherwise you could not supply, surely that does amount to a transfer of so much of your banking capital from London to the country?

It is rather more the payment of a debt due by some parties in Ayrshire to some parties in London.

Mr. Kennedy is right: the operation is the mere transfer of a debt. The Ayrshire bank is creditor of a bank in London to the amount of 1000*l*., and passes its draft on London for that sum; the person or firm that takes and pays for the draft of the Ayrshire bank has a payment to make to his correspondent in London. The transactions balance each other. The ultimate balances, as between Scotland and England, must be adjusted by an increase or diminution of the funds possessed in England by the Scotch banks; and in some cases, although not frequent, nor to any considerable amount, there may be a transmission of Bank of England notes or coin.

Notwithstanding the clearness of this evidence, the following questions put by the Committee, as to the distinction between capital and currency, in the subsequent examination of Mr. Anderson, manager of the Glasgow Union Banking Company, will show the little impression produced by it on the examiners: —

2323. (*Chairman.*) Do you at all attempt to regulate your circulation by the state of the foreign exchange?

Not the circulation; we regulate our business by the state of the foreign exchanges, but we consider that the circulation does not require any regulation; *our advances and loans we regulate, but not the circulation of our notes.*

2324. Do you conceive that the circulation is sufficiently regulated by your simply answering the demands of your customers?

I think so.

2335. Do you conceive that the consequence of restraining your loans and advances is to produce any effect upon the amount of your circulation?

No immediate effect upon the amount of our circulation.

E

2336. Does it eventually?

The circulation is eventually affected by the languor that follows a pressure; when wages are low and people are out of employment, there is less money circulating among them, and our circulation is diminished, but the immediate effect of a pressure *is not to diminish the circulation.*

2337. Does then any diminution of the circulation which takes place *arise from a less demand on the part of the public, and not as the result of any greater caution on the part of the .bank?*

Exactly.

2338. (*Mr. Grote.*) But the effects you have described imply an increased demand on the part of the public at such periods for your circulation?

It is an increased demand for money *, but not for circulation.

2339. When those demands are made, in what manner do you supply them; is it not by an increase of your own notes?

In most cases an increased demand comes upon us in the shape of orders upon London, or orders upon Manchester or Liverpool; the pressure upon us is chiefly from the South, and an extra demand from London, Liverpool, and Manchester we feel as the first indication of pressure; it is not from our own immediate districts.

2340. (*Chairman.*) Do you mean that your customers have demands upon them, which it is necessary for them to discharge in Manchester, London, and other places?

Yes, that is to a considerable extent the case.

2341. (*Mr. Grote.*) In what manner do you enable your customers to make those payments which you have to make in Liverpool, or London, or Manchester?

By giving them orders upon our agents and correspondents in those places.

2342. You direct a certain portion of the funds which you have in London, or Liverpool, or Manchester to be applied to that purpose?

We do.

2343. Then, in point of fact, you make those advances

---

* It is quite clear that by *money* the witness means capital, as distinguished from circulation.

not out of your own local currency, but out *of a certain portion of the London currency* upon which you have a demand ?

No ; I think that does not precisely describe the operation. It is our capital ; it is capital which we have collected in Scotland, and placed in London for that purpose ; *it is not London currency* lent to Scotland, *but it is capital* belonging to Scotland that has been placed in London, and is now applied to the purposes for which it is wanted.

2344. But if you direct payment to be made in London, this payment must be made by means of the notes of the Bank of England, which alone circulate in London?

Of course.*

2348. When increased demands are made upon you by your customers in Glasgow, do you not answer those demands by means of your own local notes, and not by orders upon London?

Certainly ; our circulation from Tuesday to Friday, and from Friday to Tuesday again, is increased upon this occasion ; but *we do not reckon that circulation,* because we know that it is immediately to return upon us, and that it is an advance, not of circulation, but of capital ; it becomes at the next exchange-day *an advance of our capital.*

2349. You feel satisfied that the increase of notes which you might make at that period would immediately come back upon you in the exchange, and that you would be required to pay them by orders on London?

Yes; or by exchequer bills in Edinburgh.

2361. Do you not, by means of this increased amount of advances in the extraordinary periods to which the questions have alluded, add to the means of purchasing goods possessed by the persons who borrow from you?

Yes, we do.

2362. And is not that practically tantamount to *so much increase of circulation* in the local districts in which your loans take place?

I think not of circulation ; I think it is capital ; because

---

* The question and answer are both wrong. The former assumes that the payment *must* be made in Bank of England notes, and the latter acquiesces in the supposed *necessity :* they *may* be paid, and most commonly *are,* by set off at the clearing-house.

the notes we pay out are not retained for days or weeks to make the purchases, they are paid immediately to some other bank, and come back to us upon the exchange, and *they become an advance of capital* by us to the party, to enable him to make his purchases.*

2363. But although ultimately it comes to be an advance out of your capital, yet for a certain time it is an advance made by means of your circulation only, without the aid of your capital?

For two or three days it is.

2364. For a certain time, longer or shorter, as the case may be?

It cannot, I think, be longer than till the next exchange-day with regard to those extra advances.

2365. (*Mr. Gisborne.*) Practically, has it more effect *in giving power of purchasing* goods in London, than if you gave them a draft upon your banker in London?

No; I think not.

2366. (*Mr. Grote.*) But during the period which elapses between the time of your making the advance originally in your own notes, and the time when you give the order on London, in consequence of the notes coming back to you during that interval, whether it be long or whether it be short, must there not be an increase of the circulation of the country generally?

I think that brings us back to the question which has been so much discussed here, viz. whether deposits form a part of the circulation. *Those notes which we pay out do not remain out;* they must be paid back either to us or to some other bank, in the shape of deposits, till they are to be used, and *they do not increase the permanent circulation of the country,* unless for a day or two, scarcely for even a day.

2367. (*Sir James Graham.*) What proportion of the people of Scotland receiving notes employ bankers?

A very large proportion of the people of Scotland employ bankers; we have been enquiring into that since we came together. One of the gentlemen here, who is at the head of

---

* It is impossible to place in a clearer light the distinction between capital and circulation, as applied to purchases between dealers and dealers.

a bank with a large number of country branches, informs me, that the number of creditors of his bank is 20,000. In our case I have a return since I came to town, making the number in our bank 15,770 ; and one of the gentlemen who is here, and who is at the head of a bank without branches, says that he has 7000 people holding his obligations.

2368. (*Mr. Grote.*) Deposit accounts?

Yes ; deposit accounts, or current accounts bearing interest.

2369. (*Sir James Graham.*) Inasmuch as every payment into a bank, whether in the shape of a deposit, or to the credit of a current account, bears interest day by day, and inasmuch as no commission is charged upon operations on an account, and inasmuch as a great proportion of the people receiving money in Scotland employ bankers, does it not follow that every payment made in local notes finds its way almost immediately within the space of twenty-four hours into the hands of some banker?

I think it does.

2370. (*Mr. Grote.*) Would not the consequence of that proposition be, if followed out, that there should be no notes whatever in the hands of the public, but that all the notes issued by each bank should be in fact in the hands of other banks?

That is the effect. There are three millions of notes out, which is a very small amount; *people must have a certain amount of money in their pockets and boxes at home, and shopkeepers must keep a certain amount of money in their tills,* the daily receipts of their business ; *and manufacturers must keep notes to pay people's wages, and so on ;* but that altogether forms but a small proportion compared to the circulation of England. Our three millions in Scotland amount to about 1*l.* a head of the whole population ; in England, although you have a gold circulation for every thing below 5*l.,* your paper circulation amounts to 2*l.* a head. I am taking about fifteen millions for the population, and thirty millions for the currency.

The distinction between currency and capital, which is so clearly shown by these remarkably intelligent witnesses, is not a mere matter of classification or of verbal criticism. The confounding of one with the other is a prolific source of fallacy in reasoning, and of error in practical application, in questions relating to the management or regulation of banks.

Of this a striking instance was exhibited in the reasons adduced by the advocates of the currency theory, in justification of the advances made by the Bank of England in 1835, against the deposits on the West India loan. The justification proceeded on the ground that, but for those advances, *the currency would have been unduly contracted.* What the notion could be of undue contraction of the currency, that is, of an inconvenient want of bank notes in the hands of the public or of the bankers, as long as any amount might be obtained by discount at 4 per cent., passes all reasonable comprehension. The truth is, that it was wholly a question of disposable capital; and was it possible to imagine that there could be any danger of an insufficiency of it, at a time when the disposal of it was so recklessly going forward in credits to America? While as regards the circulation or currency, there is every reason to believe, on a view of the state of things at that time, that the amount would have been neither more nor less than it was, whether the advances had been made or withheld.

CHAP. X.

CHARGES AGAINST THE MANAGEMENT OF THE BANK OF ENGLAND.

THE foregoing extracts from the examinations of the country bankers give the evidence of witnesses who, while explaining the working of the country bank system, offer no opinion, adverse or otherwise, as to the management of the Bank of England. But there are witnesses before that Committee who, while giving very elaborate evidence, comprising highly interesting details, serving to exhibit what, from their regularity, may be deemed to be laws determining the variations of the country circulation, change the whole course of their reasoning when they give their opinion upon the conduct of the Bank of England.

They charge that institution with being the main cause, by undue expansion and subsequent contraction of *its issues*, of causing the alternations of excitement and depression which have characterised the commercial state of this country of late years. And a whole host of writers, some as partisans of the joint stock banks, others unconnected with any banks, are loud in their declamations against what appears in their eyes the monster monopoly of the Bank of England; contending, as they do, that whereas the country banks of issue are limited as to any power of adding to the circulation, no limitation exists to the power of the Bank of England to make any addition to its issues, which a view to the interests of its proprietors may dictate; that it can purchase exchequer bills and other government securities and bullion, and discount bills, and make advances to any amount that may suit its convenience, against *issues of its notes;* and that if then the exchanges become adverse, and its bullion goes out, it puts on the screw, to the great derangement of all commercial operations.

The evidence of Mr. Hobhouse and Mr. Gilbart furnishes striking instances of the mode of reasoning by which it is attempted to be shown that, while the country banks are perfectly powerless in any attempt to regulate their issues, the Bank of England is all powerful, and can enlarge and contract its circulation at pleasure, subject only to an ultimate limitation by the exhaustion of its treasure.

E 4

H. W. Hobhouse, Esq.

158. (*Mr. Gisborne.*) Can you state any marked distinction between the Bank of England and country bankers as issuers?

I think the banks in the country are banks of issue to a very small amount compared with the Bank of England. The Bank of England deals with nothing *but its own currency; it is always buying and selling circulation,* if I may use the expression; *it issues circulation against gold,* which I consider to be a very unwholesome thing, whether London or the country wants the circulation or not. Then, again, they lend their notes for circulation in the country, which a country banker never does; he would lose his credit if he did that: he could never hold up his head afterwards, *if he attempted to put out his circulation as the Bank of England does;* then the Bank of England are buying and selling securities, *and acting upon the circulation,* whereas the country bankers are entirely passive, and that is the great distinction which I should draw: they carry on the business of issuing to an infinitely smaller extent than the Bank of England, and therefore that is not a fair measure to judge them by.

159. (*Mr. Hume.*) Are the Committee to understand that you object to the Bank of England issuing notes for gold?

If there is no actual demand for purposes of circulation, *it increases the circulation when it is not wanted.* If a person were to come to my bank and put a quantity of gold into my bank and ask me to issue notes against it, I would not do it, for I could not make them stay out unless they were wanted; they would come back; therefore, as I say, I could not conduct my business in the same way as the Bank of England does. If a person brought gold to me I should have to pay coin for it.

160. (*Mr. Grote.*) And the person who brings to you bullion might go and get that coined at the Mint?

Yes, but if there is no demand for circulation he does not do it; but in the case of the Bank of England he puts it in for a temporary purpose, and *out come the bank notes;* it may be a very wholesome thing for the Bank of England to have that power, but I could not do it. I know that the notes would return upon me immediately; *in short, I have no power over the circulation.*

J. W. Gilbart, Esq.

1015. (*Chairman.*) What are the other tests by which you ascertain whether the issue of bank notes was or was not required?

Besides the rate of interest, I consider the amount of money in circulation, as far as regards the Bank of England, as a test.

1016. Will you explain that answer more fully?

An increase in the circulation of the Bank of England, I conceive, differs from an increase in the circulation of the country banks, because the increase of the circulation of the country banks is drawn out by the state of trade in their respective districts. The country bankers having no power to purchase stock, or exchequer bills, or bullion, with their notes, an increase of circulation by them is indicative of an increase of trade in their districts; either that there is a greater briskness of trade, and a greater quantity of commodities bought and sold, or else, from some other circumstance, there is an advance in the price of those commodities, and, therefore, I do not consider that any positive increase in the amount of the circulation of the country banks is any absolute proof of excess of issue; if that were the case, it would appear that the circulation of Ireland, which was very much larger in December, is a proof of an excessive issue of notes in that country, whereas the fact is, that a larger number of notes at the end of the year are drawn out by the produce of the harvest being brought to market. But an increase of *the Bank of England circulation* arising *from an issue of its notes against bullion*, or against purchase of government securities, would be an increase not required by trade, and would necessarily reduce the rate of interest and lead to speculation in trade, and investments in foreign securities.

1017. Do you mean, then, that any increase of issue of bank notes against bullion, or by the purchase of securities, is, in your opinion, an excess of issue?

I must again guard myself; I am very averse to universal propositions, because I believe there are no universal propositions in the science of political economy; that they are all subject to exceptions, and may be modified by circumstances. But taking it as a general rule, and, referring to experience, *I think that an issue of notes against a lodgement of bullion will be usually found to be an excess of issue.*

From the tenour of these answers it might be
inferred that every purchase of securities or of bullion
by the Bank of England is made in bank notes which
remain out and add to the amount of the circulation;
and if they do not remain out, how can they be said to
add to the circulation? As to the buying and selling of
securities, this, the Bank, having a large capital and
deposits, might do if it were not a bank of issue. But,
say Mr. Hobhouse and Mr. Gilbart, the country banks,
if they buy securities, cannot pay for them in their
notes, the demand for these being limited; they must
therefore pay for them in an order on London. But
what is that order? It enables the holder of it to get
gold for it, if he has occasion for or can make use of
the gold. And what does the Bank of England do,
more or less, when it makes advances by loan or discount, or buys securities? The seller of the securities
or the borrower may claim bank notes or gold as he
might claim Bank of England notes or gold from any
other bank of issue. But he may not, and in most
cases does not, want the bank notes or gold. He
may require only the power of passing a cheque
against the amount, which he pays into his banker.
And, in point of fact, unless there is a demand for
gold, the great bulk of the transactions of the Bank
of England, whether in the purchase or sale of securities or of bullion, is accompanied with as little effect
upon the amount of bank notes in the hands of the
public as are the transactions of the country banks
of issue.

The most extraordinary part of the charge against
the Bank of England is, that *it issues its notes* in excess
by its purchases of bullion. In the first place, there
is no more reason for supposing that bank notes of
necessity actually pass out of the Bank for purchases
of bullion than for purchases of securities; but, in the
next place, the Bank cannot help purchasing gold.

The gold comes into the Bank sometimes from the internal circulation, and in that case it is paid in as a matter of course; sometimes it comes in as bullion from abroad in the shape of sovereigns which had been previously exported, there being no seignorage; and in such case also it is quite obvious that the Bank must be passive in receiving them and in paying for them either in notes or in a book credit. But take the case of uncoined gold. If the Bank objected to buy it, it might be taken to the Mint by the importer, and when coined paid into the Bank. Mr. Hobhouse says that it would not be taken of necessity to the Mint, because there might be no want of it in the circulation. This would be true if it could only find vent in the circulation as currency, meaning for retail purposes, those being the only purposes for which coins circulate. But the importer requires the use of it as capital, and if the Bank will not buy it as bullion he must submit to the delay of having it coined, so that he might pay it into the Bank, and thus by a small sacrifice of interest get the command of his capital. The Bank, therefore, in buying the bullion at 3*l*. 17*s*. 9*d*. per ounce spares the importers this round-about process. It is, moreover, to be observed, that the Bank is by its constitution a dealer in bullion, and if it were not, some other establishment would be.

So inconsistent, indeed, are the charges against the Bank of England with reference to its supposed management of the circulation, that while the country bankers are charging it with issuing its notes in excess by purchases of bullion, the partisans of the currency principle, that is, of a metallic variation, consider it to be an imputation upon the present system or upon the management, that an import of bullion is not attended with a corresponding increase in the circulation.

CHAP. XI.

THE BANK OF ENGLAND HAS NOT THE POWER TO ADD TO THE CIRCULATION.

FROM the description which has been given (at p. 21.) of the employment of bank notes when issued and circulating out of the walls of the Bank, it must be evident that the uses of them are such, the purposes for which they are wanted so defined and limited, that in no case could the Bank, by its own volition, add one hundred thousand pounds, perhaps not one hundred pounds to the amount already in circulation among the public. I do not mean that the Bank might not enter into some spontaneous operation which should be of such a nature as to require notes to pass out of its hands without being returned on the same or the following day in the shape of deposits or of a demand for bullion. The nature of the transaction might be such as to require a lodgement of the bank notes in the exchequer or in the hands of agents or of bankers for a few days. What I do mean to say is, that the notes would, in such case, inevitably return to the Bank as deposits, or, what comes to the same thing, be idle in the tills of the bankers, without having performed any of the functions of money in the transactions of purchase or of payment, distinct from that to which they had been specifically applied. I quoted on a former occasion* an opinion of Mr. Gurney's delivered in 1833, that while the transactions of London are abundantly supplied with notes, the effect of an additional 5,000,000*l.* would be, that it would remain inoperative or rather idle in the tills of the bankers.

* History of Prices, vol. iii. p. 156.

In the evidence before the Committee of 1840 on Banks of Issue, the question of the power of the Bank to increase the circulation is raised in a form which admits of a further illustration of the negative of the existence of such power. It is to be borne in mind that the following questions and answers involve a reference to the effect of the supposed operation of the Bank of England on prices, as well as on the amount of the circulation and on the rate of interest. My immediate object in the quotation is to show that the Bank could not add by the operation to the amount of its outstanding notes in circulation.

The following questions by Sir Robert Peel, and answers by Mr. Page, had been preceded by a question which assumed the Bank to have 20,000,000*l.* of notes in circulation, and 10,000,000*l.* of coin in its coffers.

Qu. 832. Supposing the 20,000,000*l.* of notes issued upon the discount of bills of exchange or advances to government remained the same, and that the Bank were suddenly to throw 5,000,000 of sovereigns into *active circulation,* as advances upon landed securities, would there be no effect produced upon the currency of the country?

Yes, if they remained out there would be an effect on prices; but they would soon come back. There would in that case, in the first instance, be no alteration in the total quantity of money as administered by the Bank of England, but the Bank would do just what a private banker does—he would employ the money he has in deposit in the purchase of securities without increasing his liabilities; but that state of things would never last; because *either those sovereigns would be wanted in the circulation or they would not; they most certainly would not; because before that time they were never called for, and, not being wanted in the circulation, they would return to the Bank to increase the deposits,* and then the Bank would be precisely in the situation I have mentioned before; they would increase their securities and increase their liabilities.

833. They would return to the Bank because they would

have depreciated the currency; but would not they affect prices while they remained out?

They would not remain out for any length of time.

If Mr. Page had confined himself to that part of his answer which I have marked with italics he would have been correct. The sovereigns, not being wanted in the circulation, would return to the Bank to increase the deposits ; and then, if the following question, instead of " 833. They would return to the Bank " because they would have depreciated the currency ; " but would they not affect prices while they remained " out?" which assumes that they would have entered into the circulation as currency — if instead of this erroneous assumption, the question had been *why* or in what sense the sovereigns would not be wanted and would return to the Bank, the proper answer would have been, that the circulation of sovereigns is wanted chiefly, if not exclusively, for purposes of income, including wages, and of expenditure, and not as instruments for transfers of capital. It is in the retail trade between dealer and consumer that coins are principally used. Now, as it does not appear why any additional demand in the retail trade should be caused by this forced issue of sovereigns by the way of loan on mortgage, they would, in all probability, as being most inconvenient instruments for a mere advance of capital, return to the Bank as deposits.

By the supposition it is a forced operation of the Bank. In effecting its purpose of making advances to that extent on mortgage, it would have to displace the existing capital (because the hypothesis assumes that things were in a sound and quiescent state, in other words, *in equilibrio*, there being no new circumstances to induce fresh borrowers on that description of securities at the existing rate of interest) which had been previously advanced and was absorbed in mortgages. This could not be effected without a great reduction in the rate of interest on that description of securities by way of a sufficient inducement to fresh borrowers, or to the existing mortgagees to pay off their loan and to borrow from the Bank at the reduced rate.

The mortgagees being unexpectedly, and to them inconveniently, paid off, would of course seek other investments; but these they would not readily find, unless by offers of capital at a still lower rate of interest. This would only remove the difficulty of finding employment for the capital by a single step, or rather merely shift it; for whatever securities were purchased by the capitalists whose mortgages had been paid off and transferred to the Bank, would set afloat just so much capital as would be produced by the transfer of those securities.

The result would not be materially varied if the supposed advances made by the Bank on mortgage were to parties who were buying land speculatively or otherwise. There would, of course, while the operation was in progress, be a temporary rise in the number of years' purchase of landed property. In this case the sellers of the land would probably, after paying off incumbrances, seek investment for the remainder of the amount in securities at home or abroad, and would, in the first instance, with the mortgagees who were paid off, deposit the sovereigns so received at their banker's. In either or both cases, the deposits in the Bank of England or other banks would be increased. The deposits so accumulated would, by the operation of a greatly reduced rate of interest, gradually find employment as capital at home or abroad, without necessarily having in the mean time produced the slightest effect in increasing the amount of the circulation or depreciating the currency, as by the question was supposed, in any other sense at least than in reducing the rate of interest.

I have been the rather induced to remark upon the opinion of Sir Robert Peel, as conveyed by his question No. 832., because it should seem that the examinations of the Committee on Banks of Issue, of which he was a member and in which he took part, had not shaken his belief that it was in the power of the Bank, by an attempt at a forced issue, to increase the amount of the circulation either in gold or bank notes, and so to depreciate the currency. On the last day of the session of 1842, Sir Robert Peel, after remarking on the tendency of the improvements effected by his tariff to mitigate the existing distress, concluded with saying, —

" I admit that there are modes by which a tem-
" porary prosperity might be created. I might create
" a temporary prosperity by the issue of 1*l.* notes,
" and by encouraging the Bank to make large issues
" of paper ; but such a prosperity would be wholly
" delusive. It is much wiser, in my opinion, to
" abstain from the application of the stimulus." *

The effect of the issue of five millions being in 1*l.* notes instead of sovereigns would be so far, and only so far different, that although they would not, provided they were issued on securities, form an addition to the amount of the circulation, there might be such a preference on the part of the public for 1*l.* notes over sovereigns, that gold coin would go back to the Bank instead of the small notes.

It would appear from the conclusion of the speech just quoted, and from his examination of Mr. Page, that Sir Robert Peel is of opinion that a forced issue of sovereigns or of 1*l.* notes would be *most* efficacious, but that large issues of paper generally by the Bank,

* Hansard, 12th August, 1842.

under encouragement from government, would in *the next degree* be effectual, and serve as a *stimulus* in creating a temporary prosperity.

Now, whatever may be the ultimate permanent effects of a fall in the rate of interest on the prosperity of the country, it is quite clear that temporary prosperity is not the necessary or immediate consequence of a greatly reduced rate. At the time when Sir Robert Peel made the remark which I have quoted, namely, in August, 1842, the rate of interest had fallen below what it had been for several years before, and most assuredly nothing like a return of prosperity, however short-lived, had yet manifested itself. He cannot, therefore, any longer have supposed, whatever may have been his impression when examining Mr. Page two years before, the rate of interest being then still comparatively high, that mere advances on securities, that is, loans or discounts by the Bank (always assuming that the securities are unexceptionable) could have the desired effect. How he would have proposed the extra issue to be made, with the view of creating temporary prosperity, does not appear.

The object of tracing thus far the operation, hypothetically suggested by Sir Robert Peel, is to show that the Bank of England cannot, any more than the country banks, at its pleasure, or for the purpose of employing productively, that is, in securities, a larger than usual proportion of its deposits or of its bullion, cause an enlargement of the circulation ; and that the usual phraseology, by which the Bank of England and the country banks are said to enlarge their circulation as a voluntary act, is incorrect, so far as implying a power which they do not possess of directly adding to the amount of bank notes remaining out in circulation, passing from hand to hand among the public, and performing the functions of money in daily transactions.

It is possible that, coincidently with this operation of the Bank in a sudden forced advance of 5,000,000*l.* on mortgage, there might be circumstances in progress, such as an extension of trade and a rise of prices, or a state of discredit of country bank paper, which might absorb a part of the extra sum issued by the Bank; in which case a part only of that extra sum would return to the Bank, some of it as deposits, and some of it to be exchanged for notes, the gold not being wanted for internal purposes. But, under the circumstances here supposed, an increased amount of bank notes would, but for this operation of the Bank, have been called forth, either by depositors or by discounts, or by an influx of bullion.

The conclusion from the view here presented is, that neither the country banks nor the Bank of England have a *direct* power (their advances being on securities, and the paper convertible) of enlarging their circulation; and that the inference, from the mere fact of an increase or diminution of the amount of bank notes in circulation, as being an indication of a designed enlargement or contraction of issue by the Bank of England to the extent of the difference, proceeds on a false analogy by neglecting a consideration of the distinction between issues used synonymously with advances " on securities," and issues of government bank notes or assignats. It is only the latter description of circulation of bank notes which admits of being increased in amount at the will of the issuers.

CHAP. XII.

ON THE CONNECTION BETWEEN THE AMOUNT OF THE CURRENCY AND THE PRICES OF COMMODITIES.

A GREAT part of the examination of witnesses by the Committee of the House of Commons on Banks of Issue in 1840, was directed to the eliciting of opinions as to the terms by which the various kinds of instruments of exchange should be designated and classified. The witnesses were severally called upon to define the sense in which they used the terms " money, currency, and circulation," and to say whether they included deposits in the Bank and bills of exchange under any or all of these terms.

The importance which was attached to the attempt at settling those definitions seems to have arisen from an opinion which prevailed evidently among the members of the Committee*, that, by arriving at a conclusion as to what part of the various forms of paper credit should be considered exclusively as money or

---

* From the tenour of the questions which were put to me and other witnesses by Mr. Hume, it might be inferred that he was of opinion that bank notes and deposits, as they conferred *a power of purchase*, were operative as a cause of variations of prices. And it is possible that such was *then* his opinion ; but, not long before, he seems to have entertained a very different view. In the debate on Sir W. Clay's motion for a committee on Joint Stock Banks, May 12. 1836, Mr. Hume said, " With regard to the amount of paper issues, I think I could show that it would be impossible to issue too much paper money, if it were made convertible into gold in every part of the kingdom on demand. Indeed, I believe that great delusion exists in the country with regard to the effect on prices of the currency. My opinion is, that the quantity of money depends on the rise of prices ; and that the rise of prices does not depend on the quantity of money. I hold the prevailing doctrine to be extremely erroneous on this point. The currency doctors I know differ from me ; but there has never been a fair opportunity of demonstrating the truth of my propositions."

F 2

currency, conferring *a power of purchase*, some criterion or test might be found of the influence of one of the principal elements upon which not only the state of trade and credit, but also general prices depend; it being assumed that commodities, although liable in each particular instance to be influenced by circumstances affecting the supply and demand, are more or less under a direct influence from variations in the quantity of money or currency. And the same assumption of a direct agency of the quantity of money, according to the assumed definition of it, on prices, will be found to be either expressed or implied in the vast majority of the numberless publications to which the currency question has given rise.*

An increase or diminution of the amount of bank notes is evidently considered, not only by the professed adherents of the doctrine of the currency principle, but by a large proportion of the public who take an interest in the subject, to be analogous, in the effects on markets, to alterations in the quantity of a government compulsory paper; or, in other words, they consider that prices in such cases are under a direct influence from, and affected in the same manner by, variations in the amount of bank notes in circulation, which they designate indiscriminately as paper money.

This erroneous impression arises from a neglect of the consideration of the difference in the manner and purpose of the issue. I have not met with an instance in the inquiry by the committees, or in the numerous publications which have appeared on the subject of the currency, of any attention having been paid to this particular point. Indeed, the context in all of them seems to assume that there is no difference, and that therefore any attempt at explanation would be a work of supererogation. Thus,

---

* See Appendix (A).

Mr. Porter who, in the chapter on Currency, in his highly valuable work " On the Progress of the Nation," attributes to the amount of the circulation great influence on prices, contents himself with observing, " *It is not necessary to explain,* at any length, *in what manner* excessive issues of currency tend to raise the general prices of goods." * Now an explanation, however brief, of this point was exactly the thing wanted. And I cannot help thinking, that if he had suffered himself to pause and reflect upon it, he could hardly have failed to modify the opinion he has there expressed of the influence of the amount of the currency on prices, and he would possibly have been led to distrust the correctness of the view presented by the table which he has inserted in illustration of his opinion of that connection.

A moment's consideration will serve to show the importance of the distinction to which I have here alluded.

When a government issues paper money, inconvertible and compulsorily current, it is usually in payment for —

1. The personal expenditure of the Sovereign or the governing power.
2. Public Works and Buildings.
3. Salaries of Civil Servants.
4. Maintenance of Military and Naval Establishments.

It is quite clear that paper created and so paid away by the Government, not being returnable to the issuer, will constitute a fresh source of demand, and must be forced into and permeate all the channels of circulation. Accordingly, every fresh issue beyond the point at which former issues had settled in a certain rise of prices and of wages, and a fall of the

---

* Progress of the Nation, vol. ii. p. 225.

exchanges, is soon followed by a further rise of commodities and wages, and a fall of the exchanges ; the
depreciation being in the ratio of the forcibly increased amount of the issues.*

It will hence appear that the difference between
paper money so issued and bank notes such as those
of this country consists, not only in the limit prescribed by their convertibility to the amount of them,
but in the mode of issue. The latter are issued to
those only who, being entitled to demand gold, desire
to have notes in preference ; and it depends upon the
particular purposes for which the notes are employed,
whether a greater or less quantity is required. The
quantity, therefore, is an effect, and not a cause of
demand. A compulsory government paper, on the
other hand, while it is in the course of augmentation,

* Discredit is not an essential element in variations of the value of
an inconvertible paper, nor is depreciation always a necessary consequence
of inconvertibility. The notes of the Bank of England, and of the private
banks of this country, were, for two years after the restriction, of the same
value as if they had been convertible, and never experienced any discredit.
There were great fluctuations in the credit of the paper money of the
United States of America during the war of independence, and also in
the case of the French assignats, arising from fluctuating opinions as to
the chances of redemption ; and both descriptions became ultimately
valueless by excess, when all prospect of redemption had ceased. But
the Russian government paper, although, during the progress of its depreciation, by successively increasing issues, no certain or probable
prospect of redemption had been held out, seems never to have suffered
any discredit ; and the variations of the exchanges beyond those produced
by the mere excess of the paper, were such only as are incidental to
variations in the state of trade. The effect of increased issues so made
was exactly analogous to a progressive deterioration of the coin. The
depreciation of the paper reached 75 per cent. At this point it stopped,
and the government, by requiring payments for customs and other taxes
to be made in the proportion of four paper rubles to one silver ruble,
virtually established a degradation of the standard in that proportion,
just as if the standard in this country had been reduced to five shillings
for the sovereign. After continuing for some years at this rate of depreciation, the value of the paper was raised to 3 rs. 60 cs. for the silver
ruble ; and in 1838 a silver currency was re-established at the standard
which existed previous to the degradation, provision being made for
contracts that had been entered into *specifically* in bank notes, as contradistinguished from contracts in silver money.

acts directly as an originating cause on prices and incomes, constituting a fresh source of demand in money, depreciated in value as compared with gold, but of the same nominal value as before.

In a convertible state of the currency, given the actual and contingent supply of commodities, the greater or less demand will depend, not upon the total quantity of money in circulation, but upon the quantity of money constituting the revenues, valued in gold, of the different orders of the state under the head of rents, profits, salaries, and wages, destined for current expenditure.

Dr. Adam Smith, in the passage which I have before quoted from him (at p. 34.) observes : " The value of " the goods circulated between the different dealers " never can exceed the value of those circulated be- " tween the dealers and the consumers ; whatever is " bought by the dealers being ultimately destined to be " sold to the consumers." Assuredly, then, the prices at which the commodities have gone into consumption, the result of them constitu.ing the return for the capital expended in the production, may be considered with greater propriety than any other description as general prices.

The cost of production will determine whether and to what extent the supply will be continued, but the extent of the effectual demand, in a given state of the supply, will be measured by the prices which the consumers may be able and willing to pay. Now, the power of purchase by the consumers depends upon their incomes ; and the measure of the extent and of the exercise of such power is, as has just been observed, in that portion of their revenues which is destined for expenditure in objects of immediate consumption.

Of the revenues or incomes of the community devoted to immediate expenditure, by far the largest proportion consists of wages, from those of the skilled artizan, who gets his 5*l*. a week or upwards, to those of the day labourers and common workmen, whose earnings with their families are from 20*s*. to 7*s*. a week. Any increase, accordingly, of incomes, of which wages constitute the largest part, will raise general prices, and a fall of wages will depress them, supposing no alteration in the cost of production, or in the actual and contingent supply.

If prices of one or more articles of consumption fall from diminished demand, and continue for any length of time below the cost of production, the supplies will fall off until, in consequence of the diminution of supply, the price rises, so as again to cover the cost. Or if the cost of production is raised by permanent causes, the means of the consumers being limited, if the article is not a necessary of life, and if the supply fall off so as to raise the price, there will be a permanent falling off of the demand, and less of the article will be produced and consumed. But, given the cost of production, and barring the effect of vicissitudes of the seasons, and other casualties affecting the supply, the quantity consumed, at certain prices, which is the test of effectual demand, will, as I have said, depend upon that portion of the incomes of the different orders of the community which may be destined for expenditure in immediate objects of consumption.

As an instance of the false practical conclusions to which the currency theory leads, in the view taken of the distinction between bills of exchange and bank notes, and in overlooking, as it does, the distinguishing features of credit, and capital, and currency, and between wholesale and retail dealings, I have to cite the following passage from Mr. Norman's Letter to Charles Wood, Esq. (page 43.) proposing to show, according to his view, the usual effect of bills of exchange on price : —

" A buys cotton of B at 10 per cent. in advance
" on the previous price, payable at three months, and
" gives his acceptance for the amount. At the close
" of this period, or after one or more renewals, the bill
" must be paid out of the currency in existence; and if
" there is not enough money to sustain such a price, a
" fall in prices must ensue, and B will suffer from his
" bargain. But further, if the advanced price has
" become general, a stimulus will be given to the
" importation of cotton, a check to its exportation, or
" to that of articles manufactured from it, and the final
" result will probably be a fall below the original price,
" commensurate with or perhaps greater than the
" original rise. This imaginary case may be taken as
" a fair representation of *the usual effect* of bills of
" exchange on price."

The bills of exchange are here supposed to have
an effect on price, that is, to be a cause of price;
whereas *the very reverse is the fact.* The bills of
exchange, so far from being a cause, are the effect
of price. *The prospect of advantage supplies the
motive, and the credit of the buyer constitutes the
power of purchase,* while the bill of exchange is a
mere written evidence or acknowledgment of the
debt, accompanied with a promise to pay the amount
at some definite period. If A, the buyer at the
advanced price, has not under-estimated the supply,
or over-estimated the consumption, the manufacturer
must give the advanced price, and, by his acceptance
or cheque, enable A to discharge his acceptance at
the time of its becoming due, with a profit, or by
the supposition, without loss. But if A has been
mistaken in his view of the supply, actual and contingent, compared with the rate of consumption, the
price will fall, and he will suffer from his bargain;
and if he trades upon a large proportion of borrowed
capital and the loss be heavy, he will fail.

So much of the results, in the alternative of the

two suppositions, is clear enough according to the ordinary course of business. But, according to Mr. Norman's view, if I understand it rightly, the price would fall, not because the buyer had been mistaken in his view of facts and in his reasoning as to the supply relatively to the rate of consumption, but *because there was not enough money to sustain the advanced price.*

Mr. Norman does not attempt to show that the quantity of money requisite to sustain the advanced price of cotton in the case supposed is necessarily dependent on the aggregate of coin and bank notes, which he considers as the currency in existence in the country, and out of which he states that the bill given by the buyer of the cotton must be paid. He seems not to be aware that the quantity of money applicable to the purchase of cotton and cotton goods from the raw material in the hands of the grower, to the finished article in the hands of the consumers, is dependent upon that portion of the money incomes of the consumers at home and abroad, which they are able and willing to expend in the satisfaction of their wants for cotton clothing and the other uses of cotton goods. All sales and purchases from those of raw cotton in the hands of the planters, till the finished goods find their way into the hands of the consumers, must in the aggregate reach that amount, and cannot but by miscalculation of employers of capital and labour, in the distribution and the manufacture through the intermediate stages, exceed that amount, whatever may be the multiplication of bills arising out of the intermediate transactions.

The principle of limitation, therefore, to the maintenance of an advanced price of any particular article, in consequence of actual or apprehended deficiency of supply, *is not the quantity of money in existence in the country,* but *the quantity of money in the hands or pockets of the consumers destined for expenditure in that article.* And the eventual fall of price will not be from deficiency of the quantity of currency in the country to sustain the advance, as supposed in the foregoing passage, but from the inability or unwillingness of the consumer to pay the advanced price, and from a restoration, actual or expected, of the usual or a greater supply.

But then follows a passage which shows that in that which I have just quoted, the effect ascribed to bills of exchange on prices is supposed to arise from the circumstance, not of their creation, but of their changing hands by indorsements: " A large propor-" tion of bills are drawn and paid which *have no effect* " *on the currency whatever.* Thus let A sell coffee to B " at three months, and at a fair current price, draw for " the amount, and keep the bill in his portfolio until " due; it is clear that the result will be the same as if " he had given a simple credit for the same period. " The economy in the use of money will commence " when he makes a payment to C by means of an in-" dorsement, and will be repeated as often as the bill, " by a repetition of this process, changes hands. Thus " even purchases on credit, at advanced prices, against " which bills are drawn, *may be made without any new* " *creation of money,* and without the necessity of em-" ploying an economising expedient."

The *advance in the* price paid for cotton in the first of the hypothetical cases stated, and *the fair price* at which the coffee is in the second case supposed to have been sold, should seem upon the face of the statements to be essential conditions of the cases; but the two concluding sentences are calculated to remove that impression, and to lead to the inference that the prices paid have had nothing to do with the question, how far bills of exchange do or do not answer the purposes of money *in a supposed effect on prices.*

The cases only prove what I have before endeavoured to show, that purchases and sales between dealers and dealers may be, and are in a great majority of cases, transacted through the medium of credit, of which bills of exchange are the written evidence; the successive indorsements adding to the credit of the original names on the bills, and serving the purpose of so many transfers of capital. And I have only referred to the cases stated by Mr. Norman as bearing on the question of the connection of the currency with prices, in order to point out the grave error of his doctrine, in ascribing to bills of exchange an effect *on* prices, instead of viewing them as an effect *of* prices.

The same error, being no less than that *of substituting cause for effect*, is observable in a still greater degree (because more importance is attached to it) in the influence ascribed by the currency theory to the amount of the circulation, that is, of bank notes, on prices. It is an error which perverts the reasoning, and distorts the view of facts, in every attempt to apply the theory of the currency principle to the actual course of commercial affairs.

CHAP. XIII.

ON THE CONNECTION BETWEEN THE RATE OF INTEREST AND PRICES.

On the Stock Exchange, and in the Money Market, the term money is used synonymously with capital. Abundance and cheapness of money mean abundance of capital seeking employment, and a low rate of interest as the consequence; as, on the other hand, scarcity of money, and tightness of the money market, mean comparative scarcity of disposable capital, and a consequent advance in the rate of interest. And when confined to operations on the stock exchange or in the money market, the terms so applied being technical and perfectly understood among the parties using them, lead to no inconvenience either in practice or in reasoning. But, in all general reasonings on the subject of the currency, and in the application of them to proposed regulations of banking, the ambiguity of the term value of money or of the currency, when employed indiscriminately as it is, to signify both value in exchange for commodities, and value in use of capital, is a constant source of confusion: accordingly, in many of the writings on the subject, and in much of the evidence given before the Banking Committee, abundant instances may be found in which parties using the terms appear to have their minds floating between the two meanings, and to come in consequence to any thing but clear conclusions.

I will not here stop to point out the fallacious inferences to which, on the general subject, this ambiguous use of the terms necessarily leads. My immediate purpose is to remark upon it only as relates to the inquiry how far the abundance or scarcity of money, in the language of the money market, or in more correct and less mistakeable terms, a low or high rate of interest, is calculated to exercise a direct influence on the prices of the commodities. The commonly received opinion is, that a low rate of interest is calculated to raise prices, and a high rate to depress them. Mr. Gilbart in an article in the Westminster Review for January, 1841, thus explains the effects which he ascribes to the abundance or scarcity of money in the stock exchange and money market use of the term, meaning capital : — " Speculators and

" merchants have always some peculiar reason for
" dealing in one commodity rather than another; but
" the facility of obtaining the *money* (*i. e.* the use of
" capital) is the moving cause of the speculation, and
" the price of each commodity will advance according
" to the quantity of money brought to bear on that
" particular market." So far from its being true that
the facility of obtaining money (always understood
on sufficient securities) *is the moving cause* of speculation in commodities, Mr. Gilbart would find it
difficult to point out a single instance where the mere
facility of borrowing on sufficient security has been
the moving cause of any considerable speculation in
commodities.

It may be worth while, by way of exhibiting the
mode in which advances by the Bank of England,
unattended with an increase of the circulation, may
be supposed, according to the doctrine which is here
under examination, to act upon the prices of commodities, to refer to the following further extract from
Mr. Gilbart's review : —

" Again, suppose the circulation is at its proper
" amount, and the Bank should purchase a million of
" exchequer bills, the notes *thus put in circulation* not
" finding immediate employment might be returned
" to the Bank, and be lodged on deposit. *Here there*
" *would be no increase in the circulation, but an increase*
" *of a million in the deposits. A power of purchase*
" *to the extent of a million sterling* would have been
" created by the Bank, and the efforts of the depositors,
" to make the most advantageous investments, would
" have the effect of advancing the prices of commodi-
" ties, and of stimulating a spirit of speculation ; and
" should the Bank consider this increase in the deposits
" a sufficient reason for adding another million to the
" circulation, this additional million might also come
" back, and be added to the deposits ; *thus a power of*

" *purchase to the extent of two millions* would be created,
" and a spirit of speculation would be still further pro-
" moted, without any addition in the monthly returns
" to the amount of the circulation."

This might be taken for a caricature of the notion
of the *power of purchase*, which seemed to be so prevalent in the minds of some of the members of the
Committee. A power of purchase might thus doubtless be created; but why should it be directed to the
purchase of commodities if there was nothing in the
state of supply, relatively to the rate of consumption, to afford the prospect of gain on the necessary
eventual resale? The truth is, that the power of purchase by persons having capital and credit is much
beyond any thing that those who are unacquainted
practically with speculative markets have any idea
of. * The error is in supposing the *disposition* or *will*
to be co-extensive with the power. The limit to the
motive for the exercise of the power is in the prospect
of resale with a profit.

Mr. Bosanquet, in a tract entitled, " Metallic, Paper,
" and Credit Currency," containing much valuable information and ingenious reasoning on those topics,
whilst agreeing with me † as to the absence of any
direct influence of the amount of the currency on

---

* See Appendix (B).

† " I perfectly agree with Mr. Tooke that, whatever may be the increase or diminution in the amount of money, bills of exchange, or deposits, *as long as the increase or diminution shall have taken place strictly
according to the wants of the community*, variation in quantity is in no
way chargeable with variation in the prices of commodities. Prices may
rise beyond their just level (inevitably to fall again from want of demand), and the currency may increase in quantity in proportion; or
prices may be depressed from the state of markets at home or abroad
below their ordinary level, trade may become stagnant, goods may want
purchasers (inevitably to rise again from increase of demand), and the
quantity of currency may decrease in proportion; but the amount of
currency will neither be the cause of the state of prices, nor will it in any
way affect the value of money." If, instead of the lines which I have
marked with italics, be introduced the clause *as long as the paper is convertible*, I perfectly assent to that exposition of my views.

prices, attaches great importance to the influence which he ascribes to the rate of interest on the prices of commodities. At the time, however, when he wrote, which is more than two years ago (and the same remark applies to Mr. Gilbart) the rate of interest was not so low as it has since been, and it may perhaps be considered hardly fair to make use of recent experience in commenting upon opinions delivered under such different circumstances.

It is not, however, as judging by the event that I have to remark upon Mr. Gilbart's and Mr. Bosanquet's opinions on this point. My reason for referring to them is, that they state, in a manner more positive and detailed than I have met with in other writers, what they conceive to be the mode of operation of variations in the rate of interest on prices of commodities.

Mr. Bosanquet observes (p. 73.) : —

" Were the rate of interest reduced as low as 1 per " cent., capital borrowed would be placed nearly on " a par with capital possessed."

That a capital borrowed at that, or even a lower rate, should be considered nearly on a par with capital *possessed*, is a proposition so strange as hardly to warrant serious notice were it not advanced by a writer so intelligent, and, on some points of the subject, so well informed. Has he overlooked the circumstance, or does he consider it of little consequence, that there must, by the supposition, be a condition of repayment ? He goes on, however, to say : —

" The demand for issues of money " (loans of capital ?), " or the means of procuring capital, would, " in such cases, be limited merely by the amount of " available security to be produced, and the effect " would be, the rise in price of all those commodities " which can in any way be turned to account so as to " produce profit."

There seems to be a strange misapprehension involved in this mode of accounting for the effect here ascribed to the low rate of interest. We must suppose that this reduced rate is general, but that good security is required; because if credit is given indiscriminately, without reasonable security for repayment, there is no recklessness of adventure that would not be entered into. Suppose, then, that the reduced rate is general, and the loans for such length of time as to admit of being extensively acted upon by the different dealers in commodities. The effect would be precisely the reverse of that which the author would anticipate.

A general reduction in the rate of interest is equivalent to or rather constitutes a diminution of the cost of production. This is more especially and very obviously a necessary effect where much fixed capital is employed, as in the case of manufactures, but it likewise operates in all cases where an outlay of capital is required, according to the length of time ordinarily occupied in bringing the commodities, whether raw produce or finished goods, to market; the diminished cost of production hence arising would, by the competition of the producers, inevitably cause a fall of prices of all the articles into the cost of which the interest of money entered as an ingredient. And the presumption accordingly is, that the very reduced rate of interest which has prevailed within the last two years must have operated as one of the contributing causes of the great reduction of prices of some of our most important manufactures which has occurred coincidently with reduction in the rate of interest.

It is probable, however, that Mr. Bosanquet, in his theory of high prices as a consequence of a low rate of interest, may be under the influence of the same opinion as that of Mr. Gilbart and many others — that a facility of borrowing at a low rate of interest not only confers the power of purchasing, but

affords the inducement—applies *the stimulus* to speculation in commodities. If by facility of borrowing
he meant a laxity of regard to security for repayment
on the part of the lender, there is every probability
that money so borrowed will be hazardously, if not
recklessly employed; and whether in the purchase of
shares, or of foreign securities, or of merchandize, or
in any other mode of adventure or enterprise, or in
mere personal expenditure, is a matter of chance, depending on the disposition and views of the borrower;
such borrowers are not *stimulated* to purchase commodities speculatively, merely because they can borrow
on low terms; they are but too happy if they can
borrow at all. But to suppose that persons entitled
to credit are likely to be induced—*stimulated* is the
favourite term—by the mere circumstance of a low
rate of interest to enter into speculations in commodities (using the term speculation in its obnoxious
sense), argues a want of knowledge of the motives
which lead to such speculations. These are seldom if
ever entered into with borrowed capital, except with a
view to so great an advance of price, and to be realized
within so moderate a space of time, as to render the
rate of interest or discount a matter of comparatively
trifling consideration.

In truth, the importance attached to speculations in
commodities, whether as connected with bank notes, or
with the rate of interest, or with expansions and contractions of the Currency, in whatever sense these
terms are used, is greatly exaggerated. As long as
vicissitudes of the seasons are among the ordinances of
Providence, and as long as political and fiscal obstruc-
tions to the freedom of commercial intercourse are
among the errors of legislation, aggravating all other
causes of fluctuation, and among these the sliding-scale
of our Corn Laws in a pre-eminent degree, there will,
in any state of the Currency, be speculation, which, in

its obnoxious sense, implies an exaggerated view of a
deficiency of supply, and of the probable effect of it on
prices.

Not only in the view which Mr. Bosanquet takes
of the effect of variations in the rate of interest on
prices, but in the influence which he ascribes to those
variations on the state of trade and of credit, I differ
from him most widely. Agreeing with him as I do
in his argument against some of the prominent as-
sumptions involved in the currency theory, nothing,
in my opinion, can exceed the inconsistency of
reasoning, and the unfounded supposition of facts,
upon which he grounds his belief (p. 108.), that in
the attempts on the part of the Bank to rectify the
exchanges, a variation is sometimes effected in prices
of from 25 to 50 per cent. He, in this instance, takes
for gospel the assertion in the report of the Manchester Chamber of Commerce, published at the close
of 1839, that the revulsion of credit and of prices in
1837 had entailed a diminution in the value of commodities to that extent. And with the framers of the
report he ascribes that revulsion of credit and fall
of prices to the measures of the Bank of England, in
discountenancing the paper of the American houses,
and in raising the rate of discount.

As to the revulsion of credit, it was a necessary
effect of the previous undue and extravagant extension of it. But what I have to remark upon is
the assumption that the raising of the Bank rate of
discount, in 1836, to $4\frac{1}{2}$ per cent., and ultimately to
5 per cent., had a considerable influence in depressing
prices. Now if this advance in the Bank rate of discount were to be considered as the main cause, or even
a materially contributing cause, of the fall in the prices
of commodities at that time, how was it that an
advance in the rate of discount by the Bank of
England in 1839 to 6 per cent. had not any such

depressing effect ? There was a great feeling of
uneasiness, and even of alarm, through the summer
and autumn of 1839, and yet not the slightest depressing effect from these combined circumstances
was felt in the prices of produce. Circulars of
brokers and merchants are usually published at the
close of the past and the commencement of the
coming year; and in some of those of the 1st of
January, 1840, it was stated as a matter of wonder,
that though the value of money (meaning the rate of
interest) had advanced 50 per cent., that is, from 4 to
6 per cent., the markets for produce had been so well
maintained. *

There was, moreover, during the whole period of
pressure on the money market (by which is meant an
advanced and unusually high rate of interest), a remarkable absence of commercial failures of any magnitude; whereas the progressive fall in the rate of
interest from the commencement of 1840 to the close
of 1842, when it reached its lowest point, was accompanied by a marked fall in most of the leading articles
of consumption (the greatest depression of prices coinciding with the lowest rate of interest, viz. $1\frac{1}{2}$ per
cent.), and by numerous failures, among which were
mercantile and banking firms of considerable importance. A fall in the rate of interest between 1818 and
the close of 1822, was accompanied by a still greater
fall in the prices of commodities; and instances without end could be multiplied to the same effect. It is
not easy, indeed, to imagine evidence of facts more
decisive, than those which can be adduced of the
negative of the direct influence ascribed to a low rate
of interest in raising the prices of commodities, and
vice versâ. The theory is not only not true, but the
reverse of the truth.

* Appendix C.

The rise of prices in 1835-6 was mainly the conse-quence of an extraordinary demand, arising from a spirit of speculation which had its origin in America, and to which an infatuated confidence of the houses here in that trade, ministered by unbounded credits. A collapse of credit, as the ultimate result of such a previous inflation of it, is so obviously an inevitable consequence, as to supersede any call for explanation.

But, in truth, both the currency theory, and the money market theory, that is, on the one hand, the theory which connects prices with bank notes, and, on the other hand, the theory which connects them with the rate of interest, are equally in error.

The phenomena of the great fluctuations of prices which they attempt, in the face of all facts and of all correct reasoning, to account for by the supposed in-fluence of bank notes, or of the rate of interest, are those of credit, too easily and extensively given in the first instance, and withdrawn of necessity in the end with more or less violence, according to the previous greater or less undue extension. The alternations of excessive extension of credit under the influence of exaggerated opinion, with the subsequent more or less violent contraction, are, by the convenient ambi-guity and laxity of the phraseology which is in use in discussions on this subject, more, perhaps, than on any other, termed *expansions and contractions of the currency or of the circulation.*

Nothing, indeed, can be more convenient in argu-ment than this ambiguous phraseology as a ground, whether of attack or defence of the management of the Bank of England, or of the country banks, or of the present system of banking generally (with a view to the substitution of some other system), in order to prove, according to the sense in which the term cur-rency is used, that the mismanagement of one or other of these is the cause of all the mischief of which the public thinks itself entitled to complain.

There is one further remark before dismissing the question of the connection of the currency with prices which it occurs to me to make, and that is, that with the same laxity of language as is observable in all discussions on this topic, the term prices is often applied indiscriminately to commodities and to securities including shares. Now it must be quite obvious, that these two descriptions of objects of purchase are acted upon by a low rate of interest in an exactly opposite direction. A low rate of interest is almost synonymous with a high price of securities; while, as I have shown, its necessary tendency is to reduce the prices of commodities by diminishing the cost of production. And in point of fact, the phenomena of the last three years have exhibited a rise in the prices of the public funds, and of shares and of securities generally, and a fall in the markets for commodities.

CHAP. XIV.

DISTINCTION BETWEEN ISSUING AND NON-ISSUING
BANKS.

We have thus seen, that neither the amount of the circulation (bank notes) nor the rate of interest or discount, to the extent to which it has hitherto varied can be considered as exercising a direct influence on the prices of commodities, but that the greater part, if not the whole of the fluctuations of prices which are over and above those that are necessarily incidental to the nature of the commodities, are attributable to the expansion and contraction of credit, under the influence of the opinion of dealers or speculators, more or less exaggerated, of the prospect of markets.

Credit, in its most simple expression, is the confidence which, well or ill-founded, leads a person to entrust another with a certain amount of capital, in money, or in goods computed at a value in money agreed upon, and in each case payable at the expiration of a fixed term. In the case where the capital is lent in money, that is, whether in bank notes, or in a cash credit, or in an order upon a correspondent, an addition for the use of the capital of so much upon every 100*l.* is made to the amount to be repaid. In the case of goods the value of which is agreed in terms of money, constituting a sale, the sum stipulated to be repaid includes a consideration for the use of the capital and for the risk, till the expiration of the period fixed for payment. Written obligations of payment at fixed dates mostly accompany these credits, and the obligations or promissory notes after date being transferable, from the means by which the lenders, if they have occasion for the use of their capital, in the shape whether of money or goods, before the expiration of the term of the bills they hold, are mostly enabled to borrow or to buy on lower terms, by having their own credit strengthened by the names on the bills in addition to their own. A great proportion of the vast transactions of the country among wholesale dealers are carried on by credit, simple and direct for the most part in its origin, however ramified and complicated in some of its subsequent processes.

It is quite clear that credit as between dealers and dealers (including in this term, merchants, manufacturers, and farmers), however liable to occasional abuse, does not admit of being regulated by any legislative interference. But it is charged against our banking system, on its present footing, that it is, if not an originating, a very powerfully aggravating cause of the violent variations of credit to which the commerce of the country is occasionally exposed. And to some extent the charge must be admitted. There is no doubt that banks, whether private or joint stock, may, if imprudently conducted, minister to an undue extension of credit for the purpose of speculations, whether in commodities, or in overtrading in exports or imports, or in building or in mining operations, and that they have so ministered not unfrequently, and in some cases to an extent ruinous to themselves, and without ultimate benefit to the parties to whose views their resources were made subservient, is unfortunately but too true.

According to the general opinion founded on the prevalence of the theory of the currency principle, it is to banks of issue mainly, if not exclusively, that the charge here stated is made to apply. And the House of Commons appears to have been under a full persuasion to this effect, when it appointed a Committee of Inquiry into the subject of banking, having named for its object Banks of Issue. The question which I now therefore propose to examine, is to what extent this opinion may be considered to be well founded.

It is, I conceive, impossible, upon a view of the evidence before the committee in 1841, on the part of the country banks, of which I have given extracts, to resist the force of the conclusion that the amount of notes which can circulate in a given district is strictly determined and limited by the wants of the neighbourhood, so that it is not in the power of any one or more of the banks, or of all of them together, to add to the total amount of notes in the hands of the public within that district; nor, unless by substituting

Bank of England notes or coin, *directly** to diminish the amount of local notes. If this be true, and that it is so rests, as it seems to me, upon facts and reasoning so clear as not to leave room for the shadow of a doubt, what becomes of the distinction set up by the currency theory, between issuing and non-issuing banks in the power of the former as compared with the latter, to influence and disturb the amount of the circulation ?

The following passages in Mr. Norman's letter to Mr. C. Wood present an elaborate view of the supposed difference of the inducement and power of banks in a purely metallic circulation (being the same as non-issuing banks) to make advances, and thereby influence prices, as compared with banks that have the power of creating, as it is termed, paper money in aid of their other business.

" It is plain that it *would never be the interest of any body to issue metallic money in excess,* because the coin can never exchange for a greater amount of commodities than the metal of which it is formed has cost, plus the seignorage, if a seignorage be taken, *it yields therefore, in ordinary circumstances, no profit.* With bank notes the case is widely different; they yield a very considerable profit, and it is the interest of their issuers *to keep in circulation as large an amount as possible.* Hence one source of the danger of *an over-issue.* Another is

---

* I use the term " directly," because after a period in which there has been a pressure on the money market, and the banks generally have curtailed their advances, a state of languor (as Mr. Anderson in his evidence, p. 50., observed) is apt to supervene, and to be attended with diminished transactions, and a consequent reduction of the amount of bank notes. So, on the other hand, after a period in which a low rate of interest and revived confidence and extended credit have been in operation for some time, the consequent increase of transactions would probably require to be followed by an increased amount of bank notes in the hands of the public. I say probably, not necessarily, because in 1835, notwithstanding the unbounded confidence and extension of credit which then prevailed, there was no extension, and, if any thing, a reduction of the amount of notes in circulation. In every case they are a consequence, and not a cause.

found in the bodies from which they emanate. In this country the banks of England and Ireland, joint stock and private banks, are not merely *creators*, but also bankers in the proper sense of the term, *dealers in money*, and in this capacity they are exposed to a strong *temptation* to avail themselves of their privilege as issuers in aid of the other branch of their business. When the prices of goods rise, or when there is a struggle in progress against an impending fall of prices, the customers of a banker usually call upon him for increased assistance which it is difficult for him to refuse, while if at the same time interest rises the prospect of enlarging his profit is an additional inducement for him to enlarge his advances, *and to aid his banking resources by an augmentation of his circulation.* Now a rise in prices frequently precedes an unfavourable state of the exchanges, and a struggle against a fall of prices and an advance in the rate of interest, are its ordinary concomitants. Thus we see that the first stages of an export of treasure are generally characterised by circumstances which tend to cause an augmentation of bank notes, while with a metallic currency they would necessarily be accompanied by a reduction in the circulation, as in that case all the coin exported would be taken from it. It appears, then, that with a mixed currency, like that which exists in this country, the tendency of things when the exchanges are unfavourable, is exactly contrary to what would occur had we only coin. During a favourable exchange it is equally so. Further, with a metallic currency *the gold imported would be added to the circulation,* while at present in such a state of things prices fall, and the rate of interest being usually low, loans are redeemed, advances are paid off, and the paper circulation is thus kept down. The experience of the last few years furnishes us abundance of facts confirmatory of this theoretic view of the subject." *

The passages in this extract marked with italics appear to me to involve ambiguity of meaning in the terms and fallacy in the reasoning. The proposition involved in the very first sentence is untenable. It undoubtedly might be occasionally the interest,

* See also " Reflections, &c." by S. J. Loyd, p. 45, &c.

real or fancied, of bankers dealing only in metallic money, to issue it in excess. Supposing all the deposits received by a banker to be in coin, might it not be his business then, as now, in consideration of his care and trouble in keeping the cash and answering the depositor's drafts, to employ so much of the deposits as by experience he computes may not be immediately wanted by the depositors, in loans and discounts? How then can it be said that the issue of metallic money in ordinary circumstances yields no profit? And can it with truth be maintained that he cannot issue it in excess? Is he not just as much as the issuing banker, exposed to the importunity of customers, whom it may be impolitic to refuse, for loans or discounts, or to be tempted by a high interest? and may he not be induced to encroach so much upon his deposits, as to leave him under not improbable circumstances, unable to meet the demands of his depositors? Would not this be issuing metallic money in excess? In what respect, indeed, would the case of a banker in a perfectly metallic circulation differ from that of a London banker at the present day? He is not a creator of money, he cannot avail himself of his privilege as an issuer in aid of his other business, and yet there have been lamentable instances of London bankers issuing money in excess.

But, says the theory, it is the interest of issuers of notes to keep in circulation as large an amount as possible; granted; but have they the power as well as the inclination to add to the amount of their notes in the hands of the public at any given time, and thus " to aid their banking resources by an augmentation of their circulation?" The supposition of their having the power, implies, as I have before observed, a lurking impression of similarity in the *issue* between a convertible and an inconvertible paper. The issuer of inconvertible paper has the power up to the limit of utter worthlessness; while there are, as has been incontrovertibly shewn, narrow and impassable limits, totally independent of the foreign exchanges, to the power of issue of a strictly convertible paper. Admitting, although with qualification, as matters of fact "that a rise in prices frequently precedes an unfavourable state of the exchanges, and that a struggle against a fall of prices and an advance in the rate of interest are its ordinary concomitants, and that the first stages of an export of treasure are generally characterised by circumstances which tend to cause an augmentation of bank notes." I am not only not prepared to admit "that with a metallic currency they would necessarily be accompanied by a reduction in the circulation, as in that case all the coin exported would be taken from it;" but I have no hesitation in stating it as my opinion, that in the early stages of a rise of prices, and for a limited time there would, with a metallic currency, be an increase in the circulation of coin notwithstanding an incipient export of bullion*; such export of bullion not being necessarily or probably "so much coin taken from it;" nor during a favourable exchange "with a metallic currency would the gold imported be added to the circulation" any more than it is now. And I utterly deny that "the experience of the last few years furnishes abundance of facts *confirmatory* of the theoretic view of the subject as set forth in the foregoing extracts." I admit some of the facts, but no part of the hypothetical contrast, upon which the theory is founded.

In corroboration of my views on this point I avail myself of the authority of a very accomplished writer,

---

* If asked whence the increase of coin could come, the answer is, from the reserves of the bankers; who, if they could not answer all the demands upon them by depositors, must stop payment.

who unites with the practical experience of a banker a rare power of philosophical and scientific exposition; I mean the author of an Essay on value, On the Formation of Opinions, &c. In a tract entitled " A Defence of Joint-Stock Banks and Country Issues," he observes, p. 85. : —

" If the country banks have erred at all, it has not been in their conduct as banks of issue, but in their conduct as banks for discounts and loans; a matter altogether different and distinct, with which the legislature has no more to do than with rash speculations in corn or cotton, or improvident shipments to China or Australia.

" These two things are often confounded, and many of the evils which have been attributed to mismanagement of the circulation, to improper and excessive expansions and contractions, have in reality proceeded from improper discounts and loans, — transactions which would take place under any system whatever, and the evils of which can be remedied only by a progress in intelligence. On this distinction, indeed, being properly understood and kept in view, will depend, in a great measure, the wisdom of any decision which may be come to relative to the great question of a single Bank, or a multiplicity of Banks of issue.

" No one would be mad enough to attempt to interfere in any way with the management of establishments for borrowing and lending money, and yet it is not too much to say, that in that character banks are of far greater importance to the community than the other; that they produce far more extensive consequences by the regulation of their loans than they can produce by any fluctuations which they have the power of effecting as banks of issue, so long as their paper is convertible. Whatever arrangements consequently are adopted in regard to the currency, the principal sources of good and evil in the system of banking will continue.

" Supposing country issues to be suppressed, and no paper but that of one single issuer to be allowed, the banks would still be at liberty to make any loans they might think proper. All the effects, whether good or bad, produced on the commerce of the country by banking institutions would remain, except those which are specifically occasioned by local paper. Banks properly conducted would then be of the highest service to commerce as they are now, while banks improperly conducted, making immoderate and unwarrantable advances for improvident undertakings, and risking their money on hazardous or worthless securities, would bring great evils both on themselves and on the community, just like any other mercantile establishments in the hands of bad managers.

" It is necessary, therefore, in order to arrive at sound conclusions on the questions before us, not to mix up the benefits and evils of the trade of borrowing and lending capital, with the specific effects of issuing promissory notes."

And yet seeing so clearly as he does this distinction between the business of loans and discounts and that of issue in the case of the country bankers, he seems to lose sight of the distinction when he refers to the effects of the management of the Bank of England. He says, p. 62., when comparing the character and position of the Bank of England with country banks, " The former, in order to put out an additional amount of paper, has merely to purchase securities to that amount, while the latter have no direct means whatever of effecting an expansion." Now I have shown, as I trust satisfactorily, that the Bank of England has no more *direct* power in this respect than the country banks.

The only plausible argument that I have met with for a distinction between issuing and non-issuing banks, in their tendency to issue *money* in excess (meaning, if translated into correct language, "to make advances of capital in excess"), is, that in the competition, either of new Banks of Issue, to get a portion of the existing circulation, or of established banks to get an increased share at the expense of neighbouring banks, they are induced, with a view of getting out their notes, to make advances to an undue extent and upon insufficient securities. This, I think, may be admitted as true to some extent; and

to this extent there may be sufficient ground for
making whatever regulations should be thought ad-
visable to guard against malversation of banks generally, more stringent as against Banks of Issue.
But the distinction, to the extent which I have here
admitted, does not affect the question of the currency
principle.

According to that principle, Banks of Issue have
the power of issuing paper money, that is, bank notes,
ad libitum up to the check of convertibility, in giving
accommodation to their customers, beyond the ordinary
resources of their banking business. Now, so far
from this being the case, namely, that the power of
issue has come in aid of their resources, the truth is,
that in all the flagrant cases of mismanagement of
banks, the resources of the business, that is, the
deposits and the capital of the shareholders or
partners, have been brought in aid of the efforts to
get a share of the existing circulation, not to add to
it, for that was impossible. But it is doubtful, to say
the least of it, whether, in point of fact, the more
striking instances of excessive advances were in any
degree owing to their being the means of getting into
circulation an additional amount of notes.

In the case of the Northern and Central Bank,
which was a striking instance of a recklessly managed
establishment, their liabilities were said to exceed
1,600,000*l.*, while their circulation was somewhat
under 300,000*l.* Now the presumption is, that although their advances were beyond all doubt in great
excess, their issues, meaning their notes which remained out, were not excessive; that is, did not
exceed the necessities of the circulation; or, in other
words, the amount that would have been in circulation, if, for instance, Bank of England notes only
had circulated there. A strong ground for presumption to this effect is, that the whole amount of the

notes of the Northern and Central Bank, when withdrawn by their discredit, appear to have been replaced
by an equal amount of Bank of England notes. It
was on the 1st of December, 1836, that the Bank of
England came to a determination to assist the
Northern and Central Bank, and a part of the
arrangement was to take up the circulation of the
latter. Now the circulation of the Bank of England
stood thus : —

		29th Nov. 1836.	3d Jan. 1837.
London	-	£13,556,000	£13,023,000
Country	-	3,733,000	4,074,000
		£17,289,000	£17,097,000

And I would ask whether presumptive proof can
be stronger than that this excess of the country issues
of the Bank of England, at the precise time of its
intervention for the Northern and Central Bank, was
a necessary substitute for the withdrawn notes of the
latter ?

There is, moreover, this important consideration
arising out of the view here presented, and that is,
that whereas the propounders of the currency theory
have stated it as an anomaly of the existing system,
that the country circulation has occasionally been
extended (and this has been particularly remarked
by them in regard to the very time here mentioned)
when the Bank of England has contracted its circulation, and so far counteracted the efforts of the
Bank of England to redress the exchanges ; here
was an increase of the *country issues* of the Bank
of England (not distinguished as such in the Gazette
returns) of 340,000*l.*, while the London circulation
was reduced by upwards of 500,000*l.* !

It is not, therefore, the *issues* (notes) of the
Northern and Central Bank that were in excess, but

their *advances* that were greatly so. And this, I have no doubt, would be found to be the case, if inquired into, of every issuing bank that has failed. If the issues (notes) of a Bank, however small the amount, prove to be beyond the power of the issuers to pay on demand, they are virtually in excess as soon as, on being tested by that criterion, they are found to fail in the performance of the condition on which they were issued, and which gave them their value. But as long as they continue in credit, however undeserved, and in circulation, under the impression of their being strictly convertible, the amount cannot be excessive. The *quality* may, unsuspected by the holders, be bad, when the *quantity* may not be more than sufficient to answer the purposes of convenience for which alone there is a call for any circulation or currency whatever.

In treating of Banks of Issue, as contradistinguished from non-issuing Banks, it is material to bear in mind a distinction between Joint-Stock and Private Banks of Issue, which is, that in the case of Joint-Stock Banks there has not, to the best of my recollection, been a single instance of a failure of any importance which has extended to the non-payment of the notes in circulation.

My impression is, that in most, if not in all instances, the notes of Joint-Stock Banks in the hands of the public have been paid without delay, and at all events that they have been ultimately discharged. Delay or hesitation applying only in the first instance to the depositors, while the loss has ultimately fallen, as it ought to do, upon the shareholders. In the instances of private issuing Banks that have failed, the case has so far been different that the holders of notes and the depositors have equally been sufferers. But although the failures of private Banks of Issue have (as well as those of Joint-Stock Banks) been

H

within the last two or three years lamentably frequent, the collective amount of their notes in the
hands of the public has been very inconsiderable, not
to say insignificant. So inconsiderable, as assuredly
not of itself to be allowed to weigh in any degree
worth mentioning among the reasons for the 'great
change which has been proposed in the footing of our
paper circulation by the propounders of the currency
principle, that is, of superseding all other sources by a
single Bank of Issue.

I am ready to admit that the failure of a private
issuing Bank on the grounds here stated, namely, that
the holders of notes come in only *pari passu* with
depositors, is a greater evil than the failure of non-
issuing Banks, or than the failure of issuing Joint-
Stock Banks.

But admitting, as I do, that this is an evil attending
private Banks of Issue as compared with non-issuing
Banks, or with issuing Joint-Stock Banks, it is an evil
of infinitely less importance now than when country
bank notes under 5*l.* were in circulation throughout
the United Kingdom. They are now confined to
Scotland and Ireland. The difference is immeasurably
great as relates to the suffering or hardship attending
the suspension of payments of the notes of a local
bank, between notes of 1*l.* and notes of 5*l.* and
upwards. Where the smaller notes, that is, of 1*l.*, are
issued, they circulate among the working classes of the
population. Consequently, whenever banks issuing
1*l.* notes failed, the loss fell heavily on those classes
among whom the artisans and better class of operatives
received their wages in that form. That I have not
been unmindful of the evil attending the issue of this
description of notes, as connected with the risk of
failure of the issuing banks, may be seen by the
following extract from a Tract of mine, entitled,
" Considerations on the State of the Currency," published in January, 1826.

" Whatever may be determined upon as to the expediency of providing additional security for the general circulation of the country banks, there is one part of that circulation which ought not upon any footing, or with any modification, to be any longer tolerated. I mean the notes under 5*l.* These are in every point of view a most objectionable medium of exchange. Leaving out of the question the consideration of fluctuations in the value of the currency, some protection ot the lower classes against the severe losses to which they have so often been exposed, as the holders of small notes, when the banks issuing them have failed, is imperatively called for. It is quite idle to say that the lower classes have the option of refusing to take the country notes, practically in the great majority of instances, they have not and cannot have any such option. But if there is any object more important than another, for which the government of every state has been invested with the privilege of coining money, it is that of protecting the lower classes of society, who are little competent in this particular to protect themselves, from the risk of loss in receiving their stipulated wages or other payments. And this function of the sovereignty of issuing coin, which, under the strongest sanctions, certifies to every member of the community the weight and fineness of the money, when he may be entitled to receive it, justly guarded against the interference of private individuals by the severest penalties. But by a strange inconsistency, while such care is manifested to secure the community from being imposed upon by metallic money of less than standard value, every adventurer who chooses to follow the trade of a banker is allowed to issue a spurious paper money, which having neither intrinsic value nor any adequate security for eventual convertibility, is in too many instances neither more nor less than a fraud, a fraud of which the most numerous and helpless classes and those who can least bear the loss are most commonly the victims." — *Consideration on the State of the Currency,* 1826, p. 127, 128.

At the time when these remarks were written, the amount of the circulation of one pound notes in England and Wales had been computed at upwards of five millions. The evil, therefore, of the suspension of so many issuing banks as had then recently failed was one of great magnitude, which fully justified, or rather demanded, the interference of the government and the legislature to provide a remedy, and this was most effectually done by the suppression of that objectionable class of notes. At present the entire circulation of notes of 5*l.* and upwards, issued by private banks in England and Wales, hardly exceeds in amount what was the circulation of 1*l.* notes alone prior to 1826. And however to be regretted that the holders of private country banker's notes, being now of the denomination of 5*l.* and upwards, should occasionally be exposed to loss by failure of the issuers, it will hardly be contended that their case is so important and so clearly distinct from the case of depositors, and other sufferers by the failure of Banks, as to justify, with the view of protecting them, an alteration of the whole system of issue in the Kingdom.

But as it appears that whatever the relative merits may in other respects be, as between private and Joint-Stock Banks of Issue, the circulation of the latter is much more secure, a mode of gradually substituting the issues of them for those of private Banks with the least inconvenience to the public, and without injury to existing interests, would be simply that of not granting licenses for the issue of notes to any private Banks which are not already in possession of the privilege. The notes of Joint-Stock Banks and of the Branches of the Bank of England would thus by degrees supersede those of the private Banks, and so remove one source of inconvenience from the present system.

I have noticed at some length this point, namely, the insecurity of the notes of private Banks, because it has been brought in as a make weight among the arguments in favour of a single Bank of Issue. On the grounds which have here been stated, I hold it to be utterly insignificant in that view.

I shall therefore proceed to make the few further remarks which occur to me on the currency principle, in its application to our Banking system, leaving out of the question, or leaving as a point for separate discussion by those who deem it of sufficient importance, the liability to insolvency of private Banks of Issue.

CHAP. XV.

REVIEW OF THE CURRENCY PRINCIPLE IN ITS APPLICATION TO OUR BANKING SYSTEM.

IF the views which have thus far been unfolded are admitted to be correct, it can hardly fail of being seen as a fair deduction from them, that the whole of the ground on which the theory of the Currency principle proceeds is unsound. The error of supposing that, if the currency were purely metallic, every export or import of bullion would be so much taken from or added to the quantity of money in circulation, is so obvious, so palpable, as to make it a matter of surprise that such a notion should ever have been entertained. And must it not, as an inevitable consequence, follow that it is equally an error to suppose that the paper money, if administered upon the footing proposed by the currency doctrine, of a single source of issue, having a fixed amount on securities, and beyond that, exchanging only paper against gold, and *vice versâ*, would vary in amount and value in the hands of the public, with variations in the quantity of bullion exported or imported, or in the quantity of bullion in the coffers of the Bank ?

I would not misrepresent the doctrine; but instances innumerable might be adduced from the writings, and from the examination by the Committee on Banks of Issue, of the advocates of that doctrine, that it goes to the full extent here stated; tabular statements being exhibited of the discrepancies between bullion in the Bank and notes out of it, with a view to prove, according to the occasion, sometimes against the country banks, and sometimes against the Bank of England, the charge of mismanagement. One source of their error is their imagining that, in their supposed Bank of exclusive Issue, the notes paid for gold exported must necessarily be taken from out of those circulating among the public, and that the gold imported would be taken to the Bank in exchange for bank notes, which would go into the hands of the public ; and they hold it to be the opprobrium of the present system, that this is not now the case. It must, however be clear, if I have made myself at all intelligible, that in neither case would it necessarily or generally be the case, or rather, it would be rarely so, under a single bank of issue; and, except under extraordinary circumstances, the amount of notes in the hands of the public would be nearly, if not quite, the same under one system as under the other.

It may be asked, and the question is a very natural one for those who are impressed with the notion that bank notes are operative by their amount, and who are not aware of the distinction between currency and capital, how it is that the Bank of England, or the banks collectively, if they cannot contract the circulation, (as I maintain that they cannot by any *direct* operation,) nor operate through that medium on the prices of commodities, are to be supposed to have the power of influencing the exchanges ? The answer is, that it is only by a forcible action on their securities that they can influence the exchanges, so as to arrest a drain, or to resist an excessive influx. By a forcible action on securities is meant a great advance in the rate of interest on the one hand, or a great reduction of it on the other. And the rationale of such operation on the rate of interest is, that it renders *disposable capital* in the one case scarce, and in the other abundant; forcing it *from* foreign countries in the former, and *to* them in the latter case. The effect of the *pumping in* or *forcing out* of bullion by this means is infallible; and the only practical question is of the moral, or commercial, or political considerations, which may interfere with the full exertion of the power.

A forcible operation by the Bank on its securities, in either direction, will not, of necessity, as I have shown, be attended with an immediate or direct effect on the prices of commodities. The effect, if any, can be only indirect, through the medium of credit, and dependent on the previous state of the market.

I have before had occasion to notice, in referring to the examinations of the country bankers, the confounding of currency with capital, which was observable in the questions put by some of the members of the Committee. That confusion, being traceable to the deep-seated impression which they seem to have been under, that the amount of bank notes in the hands of the public was the main point for consideration, as having a direct and an important influence on prices, and on credit, and on trade, instead of being as it is, — a mere effect or indication of the circumstances which call out and maintain that amount. The same wedded attachment to the doctrine of the Currency principle which looks to bank notes, and to bank notes only, as the *primum mobile* in our monetary system, may account for the little research which the Committee made into the causes and effects of variations in the rate of interest, and for the strange misconception which pervaded the questions relating to that point, of those of its members who took a leading part in the examinations. They seem from first to last to have looked upon variations in the rate of interest as of importance only, inasmuch as those variations might be supposed to affect the amount of the circulation.

In point of fact, the liability to variation, greater or less, in the rate of interest, constitutes in the next degree only to the preservation of the convertibility of the paper, the most important consideration in the question whether the present system, with some amendment, should be continued, or some one or other of the numerous schemes for a government or national bank should be substituted for it. Mr. Bosanquet, in his publication, to which I have alluded, entertains such exaggerated views of the disastrous effects on the commerce of the country, of a considerable advance in the rate of interest, which he seems to consider as an alteration of the value of the currency, that in his scheme for a bank or banks of issue, he would prescribe a compulsory maximum and minimum of the rate, variable between six and four per cent., according to certain rules which he lays down with reference to the exchanges: and rather than allow a forcible operation on the rate of interest, in order to stop a drain on the treasure of the Bank, he would resort first to a temporary issue of 1*l.* notes, and if that should prove insufficient, suspend the convertibility of the paper! How any well-informed person, not of the Birmingham school, could seriously propose to have cash payments suspended, rather than that the mercantile community should be subjected to some inconvenience from an advance in the rate of interest, and what he chooses to consider as a necessary consequence, a fall of prices, is to me matter of unutterable surprise. It may serve as a proof of the exaggerated views entertained in some quarters of the effects of a forcible operation on the rate of interest, and it forms a contrast to the little attention paid to that point, not only by the committee on Banks of Issue, but by the propounders of the various schemes for a government or national bank.

Now, without attaching such exaggerated importance as Mr. Bosanquet and Mr. Gilbart, and some others who oppose the currency principle do, to the effects of great variations in the rate of interest, I am inclined to think, that excepting the convertibility of the paper and the solvency of banks, which are and ought to be within the province of the legislature most carefully to preserve, the main difference between one system of banking and another, is the greater or less liability to abrupt changes in the rate of interest, and in the state of commercial credit incidental to one as compared with the other; and a careful consideration of the various plans which have been submitted to the public for carrying out the currency principle, has led to a confirmation of the opinion which I have before expressed, that under a complete separation of the functions of issue and banking, the transitions would be more abrupt and violent than under the existing system ; unless, and upon this, in my opinion, the question hinges, the deposit or banking department were bound to hold a much larger reserve than seems to be contemplated by any of the plans which I have seen.

The difference between the two systems cannot be placed in a more striking point of view than in the following passages of a printed letter which Colonel Torrens addressed to me on occasion of the opinions which I had expressed on the subject in a former work.

" The difference," Colonel Torrens says, " between us is this, you contend that the proposed separation of the business of the bank into two distinct departments would check overtrading in the department of issue, but would not check over-trading in the department of deposit; while I maintain, on the contrary, that the proposed separation would check over-trading in both departments. The manner in which the separation would have this two-fold effect will be seen by the following example.

" Let us assume that the bank holds 18,000,000*l.* of securities and 9,000,000*l.* of bullion, against 18,000,000*l.* of outstanding notes and 9,000,000*l.* of deposits, and let an adverse exchange require that the depositors should draw out their deposits in bullion to the amount of 3,000,000*l.*

" In this case, if the business of issue were mixed up with that of deposit, the drawing out of the 3,000,000*l.* of deposits in bullion would have no other effect than that of reducing both deposits and bullion by the amount of 3,000,000*l.*, while the amount of the circulation and of the securities, and the power of the bank, as its securities fell due, to continue the discount business to the same extent as before, would suffer no diminution. But let the department of issue be wholly separated from that of deposit, and the result would be widely different.

" As soon as the separation was effected the deposit department holding 9,000,000*l.* of deposits with 9,000,000*l.* of securities would be obliged to sell some part of its securities, say one-third, in order to be prepared to meet the demands of its depositors. The state of the two departments would then stand thus : —

Circulating Department.

Circulation	-	-	- £18,000,000
Securities	-	-	- 9,000,000
Bullion	-	-	- 9,000,000

Deposit Department.

Deposits -	-	-	- £9,000,000
Securities	-	-	- 6,000,000
Reserve in bank notes	-	-	3,000,000

" This being the previous state of things, the demand of the depositors for 3,000,000*l.*, in gold would produce the following changes. The 3,000,000*l.* of bank notes held by the deposit department as reserve would be drawn out by the depositors and paid into the circulating department in exchange for gold, while the directors of the deposit department, in order to recover a reserve equal to one-third of their deposits would be obliged to sell 2,000,000*l*. out of the 6,000,000*l*. held in securities. The results would be, that in the circulating department the bullion would be reduced from 9,000,000*l*. to 6,000,000*l*., and the circulation from 18,000,000*l*. to 15,000,000*l*., and that in the deposit department the deposits would be reduced from 9,000,000*l*. to 6,000,000*l*., the securities from 6,000,000*l*. to 4,000,000*l*., and the reserve from 3,000,000*l*. to 2,000,000*l*. It is self-evident that the effect of these changes would be not only a contraction of the circulation but a limitation to the power to over-trade in discount and loans."

I am willing to admit this statement as exhibiting in substance the difference between us. According to my view, as there may be variations of international payments, in other words, of a balance of trade, without any grounds for inference of alterations in the value of the currencies of the countries from which or to which such balance may be due, the presumption is, that an occasional efflux of four or five or six millions would be followed at no distant period by a fully equal reflux. Such was the case in 1828-29 and 1831-32, when the treasure of the Bank having been reduced by five or six millions was replenished without the slightest operation of the Bank on the amount of its securities, or its rate of interest. And such efflux and reflux might again take place under a continuance of the present system, provided that the Bank habitually held a large reserve, without any disturbance of the money-market, and without any influence on the amount of bank notes in the hands of the public. Now, under a system of separation, and in the position of the two departments in the case supposed by Colonel Torrens, what would be the operation of a demand for export to the extent of three millions of gold? In all probability, this demand would almost exclusively fall upon the deposit department.

This being the case, the Directors would not have a moment to lose upon the first manifestation of such demand, without taking measures for retaining or restoring the proportion of their reserve. They must sell securities, or allow the existing ones, if short-dated, to run off, and they must inexorably shut their doors to all applications for advances or discounts. This would, as Colonel Torrens justly observes, operate as a limitation of the power to over-trade in discount and loans. Most effectual, indeed, would it be, and under certain circumstances of the trade, it would operate with a degree of violence on the state of credit of which, as it appears to me, Colonel Torrens has no adequate idea. This is not to be wondered at in a writer not practically conversant with trade or banking; but that other advocates for the measure of separation, who number among them merchants and bankers, should be so unaware of it as they seem to be, does indeed surprise me. Before two or three millions of bank notes could be forcibly abstracted from the amount in circulation among the public, the pressure upon the reserves of the London bankers must be extreme. They would, of course, to the utmost extent practicable, call in their loans, and resolutely refuse further accommodation.*

Although there is no modern experience of such a

---

* It is to be regretted that the Committee on Banks of Issue in 1840, instead of expending so much time upon mere controversial points of definition, and confusing themselves and the witnesses by the ambiguous terms in which the questions were conveyed, did not see fit to examine some both of the West End and City Bankers and the money-dealers, as to such of the details of their business as, without any disclosure of their particular transactions, might have served to explain for what purposes bank notes are used, and how far it would be in the power of the Bank of England to operate directly upon the amount of the circulation.

state of things, if any merchant, banker, or money-dealer were to have the case laid distinctly before them, could any of them for a moment have a doubt as to the extremity of pressure which it would cause? I am most intimately persuaded that it would be within the mark to suppose that a rate of discount (assuming that the doors of the Bank and the ears of the Directors were inexorably closed against all applications) of 20 per cent. and upwards would, in many cases, be submitted to, and sacrifices of goods, if any large proportion were held on credit, would be made at a still greater loss. And, after all, it might be a question, whether even this effort of the Bank on its securities would be effectual in restoring its reserve *in sufficient time* to meet the exigency. This would depend entirely upon the character of its deposits. If these were strictly payable on demand, while the circumstances determining the efflux were strong and urgent, the payment of 3,000,000*l.* accompanied by forced sales of securities might prove insufficient in point of time to arrest the demand; and in this case, while the circulating department would still have 6,000,000*l.* of bullion, the deposit department would have no alternative but to stop payment. A most absurd, however disastrous a state of things. But it would be too disastrous, and too absurd to be allowed to take its course. If such a crisis were to happen, as most probably it would at the time when the dividends on the public funds became due, the Government would be imperatively called upon to interfere and prevent so ridiculous, however lamentable, a catastrophe. And the only interference that could meet the emergency would be to authorise a temporary transfer of coin from the issuing to the banking department.

The truth is, that no bank of mere deposit could undertake the Government business, involving an

annual receipt and expenditure of 50,000,000*l*., subject
to deficiency of the revenue at one time, and to over-
flow at another, with so small a reserve as 3,000,000*l*.,
whatever its other business might be; and it is difficult
to conceive how it could, without the profit of the circulation, afford the much larger amount which would
be requisite. But this is a point which it is foreign
to my purpose to discuss. What I have to observe is,
that supposing the violent effort of the Bank, on its
securities, to be effectual, there cannot be a doubt that
the violence of the effort would have been attended
with inconvenience to the public. And all this inconvenience may have been purely gratuitous, as a sacrifice to the currency principle; because the utmost demand for gold might have been satisfied by an export
of 3,000,000*l*. or 4,000,000*l*. which, under a system of
union of issuing and banking, would have been attended, as in the instances of 1828-29, and 1831-32,
with no inconvenience whatever.

But it may be asked; and here is the point; supposing that the demand for export of bullion be such
that not three or four millions, but nine or ten millions will be required to satisfy it. What then becomes of a plan of quiescence? My answer is, that
I would not be accountable for a plan of quiescence
upon an amount of treasure in the Bank not exceeding nine millions at the outset of a drain. It was an
error of the Bank in 1839, to have been perfectly
quiescent until a loss of treasure from 9,336,000*l*. to
5,119,000*l*. had taken place. And the only effort
then made was an advance of the rate of interest,
step by step, to 6 per cent.*

* Although the drain on the Bank treasure ceased after October,
1839, there was no tendency to a reflux for several months thence-
forward. And the Directors were induced in consequence, very properly, by a notice dated 15th October, 1840, to restrict the date of the
bills admissible from ninety-five days to sixty-five days. On the 3d of
January, 1841, this limitation was taken off.

This effort was altogether inadequate; a difference in the rate of discount of 2 per cent. per annum, is a trifling consideration on bills having at the utmost sixty days to run ; and accordingly, the Bank did not only not succeed by these measures in reducing its securities, but, as was inevitable as long as the door for discounts was left open, actually increased them. So that with advances on deficiency bills, the securities instead of being diminished, were actually increased by three or four millions during the greatest pressure of the drain. Still, with the aid of the credits on Paris, the drain was surmounted; and although this last resource was any thing but creditable, yet, inasmuch as the crisis was thus got over, merit may be claimed in behalf of the system for having come through with little, if any, suffering or inconvenience, commercial or financial. The markets for produce were perfectly undisturbed, there were no mercantile, or manufacturing, or banking failures of any note, and there was no great fall in the prices of public securities; so that the actual inconvenience proved to be in effect very unimportant. This exemption from suffering or material inconvenience, in surmounting the drain was, as some may think, and I among them, dearly purchased : but so it was.

Now, how would the case have stood, if the separation had existed in 1839 ?

Taking the actual situation of the Bank in January, 1839, and on the supposition of a separation of the functions, allotting twelve millions of securities (instead of nine millions, an amount obviously too low) to the circulating department, the two branches would have stood as follows : —*

* This is assumed as the position of the Bank of England in January, 1839, in a paper communicated to me by Mr. Pennington, and inserted in my " History of Prices," vol. iii. p. 279. 283., since reprinted in Mr. Pennington's Letter to Kirkman Finlay, Esq., in 1840, p. 97. As

Circulating Department.

	Securities.	Bullion.
Notes, public - £18,201,000		
Banking department 3,135,000		
21,336,000	12,000,000 *	9,336,000

Banking Department.

	Securities.	Bank Notes.
Deposits - - £10,315,000		
Rest - - 2,500,000	9,680,000	3,135,000

Upon the occurrence of the demand for gold
(which would naturally be, and was in point of fact
made, by depositors in the banking department), and
which was to the extent of a little more than a
million between January and March, it may be taken
for granted that the directors would see reason to sell
or to allow the running off of securities to the same
extent, and if they at the same time shut their doors
against discounts and advances on deficiency bills,
their liabilities would be reduced to the same extent.
The notes would be taken from the banking to the
circulating department in exchange for gold, and
leave the amount of the circulation in the hands of
the public without any alteration. And this process
might by supposition have continued till the remain-

I consider Mr. Pennington's knowledge of the principles and working of
the currency to be both profound and accurate, and as my views of the
effects of a separation of issue from banking correspond with those
which he has stated in the paper here alluded to, I am induced again
to insert it, and accordingly refer the reader to it in the Appendix (D),
with the addition of some remarks made by him on the letter addressed
to me by Colonel Torrens.

* *Note to Second Edition.* — The amount of securities proposed by
the measure laid before Parliament on the 6th of this month (May) is
fixed at 14,000,000*l.*, the difference, therefore, of 2,000,000*l.* is to be
allowed for in the reasoning in the text, which, however, would not
be materially affected in its conclusion by this alteration.

ing bank notes were transferred from the banking to the issuing department, without producing the slightest effect on the amount of the circulation in the hands of the public.

A forcible reduction, however, of the securities to the extent supposed, would doubtless have abated the force of the drain, and might possibly have overcome it; but seeing the combination of circumstances which led to that drain, it may fairly be doubted whether the effort here assumed would have been sufficient to arrest it. My strong conviction is, that it would not have been sufficient, if even it had been practicable; but I doubt whether it would have been practicable. Notwithstanding the endeavours of the directors, when their attention had been fully roused to the importance of taking measures of precaution, and notwithstanding a rise in the rate of discount and a limitation of the date of bills admissible, the securities nct only were not reduced by three millions, as I have supposed they would be under a separation, but were actually increased by three millions, partly by advances on deficiency bills. Now between a withdrawal from employment of disposable capital to the extent of three millions, and an actual advance to the same amount, is a difference of six millions. Such a reduction, suddenly effected, in the amount of available capital in the hands of the public, could not fail to be attended with very important and highly inconvenient effects. The state of credit would necessarily be deranged, as would be the markets into which credit entered largely.

But great as might be the inconvenience, it ought to be submitted to rather than that the Bank should fail in its engagements.

What I wish to impress by this view is, that by the separation, the banking department would not have time to judge of the nature and probable extent of the drain, but must take forcible measures for self preservation upon the first manifestation of it. And with only such a proportion of treasure, that is, of bank notes and coin, as has hitherto been supposed necessary to allot to it, the chances are, that under such circumstances as occurred in 1839, (as also, indeed, in 1835 and 1836,) the measures to be taken to arrest a drain, however prompt and forcible, might not be effectual in sufficient time to prevent a suspension of payment by the banking department; while, by the time gained under a system of union, and the aid to the treasure of the deposit department by gold obtained from the circulating department, the pressure might be greatly diminished, and eventually got over, without any inconvenience to the public.

But then again comes the question, What is the security that the pressure would be eventually got over, and the convertibility of the paper preserved?

I have on this point only to refer to the opinions which I have on former occasions expressed, and which all the additional light since thrown upon the subject by the mass of information contained in the Reports of the Committees on Banks of Issue, and by the currency pamphlets, and, above all, by recent experience, has tended to confirm and strengthen.

In a work published in the spring of 1838 *, I took occasion to observe, " that as far as the eventful " experience of the last fourteen years, viz. since 1824, " can serve as a guide for judgment, there appear to " be good grounds for believing that not less than " ten millions can ever be considered as a safe position " of the treasure of the Bank of England, seeing the " sudden calls to which it is liable." And two years later, in February 1840, I ventured to suggest the

---

* " History of Prices," vol. ii. p. 330.

following plan as that according to which, as it appeared to me, the circulation might be conducted with the greatest convenience to the public, and with the least danger to the convertibility of the paper:—

" The plan which I would propose is, that when " the tide of metals sets fully in again, the Bank " rate of discount should be kept so steadily above " the market rate, as progressively to reduce the " securities through that channel, without increasing " them by other investments. The effect of this " would be to insure a replenishment of their coffers " to ten millions; and with the purpose of endeavour- " ing to preserve that amount *on an average*, it would " not be expedient on the part of the Bank to take " any *active* measures for the increase of its securities. " It is not improbable, judging by the strength and " fulness of the tide with which the metals have " flowed in on some former occasions, *that the* " *amount might thus reach fifteen millions*, beyond " which, according to analogy from former expe- " rience, it is not likely that it would go. The " probability is, that in the fluctuations to which our " trade, particularly that in corn, is liable, the ex- " changes would take an adverse turn; bullion would " flow out, the market rate of interest would rise to " the Bank rate, and then it would be that the ad- " vantage of the large stock of bullion would be " felt ; because to the extent of five millions the foreign " exchanges or internal demand might be allowed to " operate upon the stock of bullion, without the " necessity on the part of the Bank to counteract that " demand by any active measures in raising its rate " of discount or selling its public securities. The " quantity of money in such case in actual circulation " would not be reduced, excepting in a small propor- " tion only, to the reduction of the amount of bullion, " because the withdrawal of deposits would, under

" the slight pressure on the money market which
" would attend a rise in the market rate of discount
" to the Bank rate, restore to the circulation an
" amount of Bank notes nearly equivalent to that
" which had been in circulation against the bullion
" taken out. In the majority of cases of the vari-
" ations in the value of our currency relative to the
" rurrencies of other countries, whether originating
" on this side or the other, the balance of payments
" would in all probability be satisfied by the export
" of that amount of bullion. If the drain, however,
" on the coffers of the Bank should, after a reduction
" to ten millions, continue so as to give reason to
" apprehend the existence of more extensive and
" deeper-seated causes of demand for the metals,
" measures might be taken for its counteraction,
" without producing alarm and disturbance of the
" money market on the one hand, or endangering an
" extreme and unsafe degreee of reduction of the Bank
" treasure on the other.

" A latitude for variation between fifteen millions
" and five millions would afford a much greater ex-
" emption from shocks on the money market than a
" variation, as it has recently been, between ten
" millions and nothing.

" That the Bank might, by a regulation of its
" securities, maintain a high average amount of
" bullion, such as has here been suggested of fully
" ten millions, cannot admit of any reasonable doubt.
" And I believe that such a regulation would be
" more easily practicable than either that of main-
" taining the securities even, or of preserving the
" bullion in any given proportion to the liabilities.
" The money market would be less liable to be dis-
" turbed than under either of the two latter alter-
" natives. The utmost alteration of the rate of dis-
" count to which the Bank might have occasion to
" resort would probably not exceed 1 per cent. ; and

" the occasions for an alteration even to that extent
" would probably be rare. A system like this would
" be less restrictive, that is, the principle of limita-
" tion would operate less rigidly under such a regu-
" lation of the bullion, consistently with a blending,
" as at present, of the issue and deposit departments,
" in the Bank of England, than by their total separa-
" tion."*

After the lapse of four years since the passage here
quoted was written, I see nothing to alter in this
recommendation. The treasure has reached the
maximum which I had contemplated; and this circumstance will render more practicable any scheme
of regulation which should have for its object the
maintenance of a high average amount of treasure.
The main objection or difficulty in the way of main-
taining so large an average amount of treasure as
ten millions, is in its unproductiveness, and its consequent drawback from the profits of the Bank; but
against this consideration must be set the greater
security of its position; and, after all, the amount is
not larger than any prudent banker would deem it
right to hold against liabilities so large and so fluctuating as those of the Bank of England.

In addition to this objection, which naturally has
great weight, I took occasion in the same work,
p. 198., from which the foregoing passage has been
extracted, to state another, which, although in my
opinion of no real weight, is so specious and popular
that the remarks which I then made upon it may
be worth here repeating.

" One among other reasons that might and pro-
" bably would be urged against any scheme involving
" so large a reserve of bullion as has here been sug-
" gested, rests on the supposition that the attracting of

---

* " History of Prices," vol. iii. p. 187.

" the extra amount must be preceeded by, and attended
" with, an undue and unnatural contraction of the
" currency, the effect of which would be, a depression
"·of prices to an unnecessary extent.

" This is a consideration with a view to the public,
" which, coinciding as the reasoning does with the
" objection on the score of profit, to a large reserve, it
" is probable weighed with the Bank directors in their
" efforts to stop the influx, and to get rid of what
" they seem to have considered the excess, of bullion,
" in the spring of 1838.   With reference to the influx
" at that time, Mr. Norman, in the tract before
" quoted, observed, —

" It is probable that an increase will be found in the treasure of the Bank, between its lowest amount last spring and
the highest just previous to the next turn of the exchanges,
of from seven to eight millions.   Now such an influx of
treasure is unnatural, and could never occur with a metallic
circulation.   Its effects, greater or less in proportion to the
error, will be accompanied in the first instance by a depression
of prices, unnecessary in extent and continued too long, and
finally by a reaction, which will occasion an equally unnecessary and faulty excess on the other." p. 91.

" Why such an influx of treasure could never occur
" with a metallic circulation, or why it should be con-
" sidered as unnatural, does not very clearly appear.
" With our very extended foreign trade, which is
" habitually conducted on the footing of a large pro-
" portion of our exports being on long credits, while
" our imports are mostly paid for at short dates, and
" with our present restrictions on the corn trade,
" there might be, as there have been, on the one
" hand, large sudden payments abroad requiring a
" considerable export of bullion before any excess of
" merchandise exported could bring returns ; and,
" on the other hand, when the demand for corn and
" for other imports, including foreign securities,
" ceased or abated, the returns for an excess of

" former exports would be coming forward, and
" bullion must in that case form, for want of other
" means, a large part of such returns. Such was the
" case in 1815—1816, in 1820—1822, and, excepting
" as regards corn, such was the case with the influx of
" bullion in 1826, and in the early part of 1838. *If*
" *the ports should be shut against the importation of*
" *corn for the next two or three years, and, at the*
" *same time, from salutary distrust or other causes,*
" *there should be a diminished demand for foreign*
" *securities, there is likely to be a strong tendency to*
" *an influx of the metals**, and it is not easy to
" understand why it should not be equally strong
" with a purely metallic variation. The Bank of
" England may doubtless, as in 1836 and 1838, by a
" competition for the investment of its deposits,
" create a renewed demand for foreign securities,
" and so stop the influx of bullion ; but so the de-
" posit department likewise might do if its functions
" were separated from the issuing department.

" But it is to the supposed unnatural depression of
" prices, ascribed as an effect of the contraction of the
" circulation which is assumed to lead to the influx
" of the metals, that my remark is directed. This
" hypothesis rests upon the currency theory of prices,
" which supposes that the contraction of the cir-
" culation, in such a case as that alluded to, reduces
" prices, and that the reduced prices force an influx
" of the metals ; whereas the contraction, or rather
" the diminution of the circulation is in such cases
" the consequence of a fall of prices from causes
" arising from the state of trade, and peculiar circum-

---

* The tendency to an influx of the metals from these causes has been
so strong, that the bullion in the Bank has exceeded the utmost amount
that I had in contemplation as within reasonable probability, being now
about 16,000,000*l.* But of this amount there is reason to suppose that
about 1,000,000*l.* may be the consequence of the light gold taken out of
circulation and replaced by notes.

" stances affecting the supply and cost of production
" on the one hand, and consumption on the other.
" As to an increased value of the precious metals,
" which might be supposed to be the consequence of
" retaining permanently an addition of fully five mil-
" lions as a reserve in the coffers of the Bank, it would,
" according to any received grounds of computation,
" amount to so very minute a per centage, as to have
" no *perceptible* influence, and may, therefore, safely
" be neglected."

The views which have here been presented for consideration, lead to the conclusion that a union of the
business of banking with that of isssue, when conducted by well regulated banks, is calculated to be
much more convenient to the public than a separation
of those functions.

Mr. Norman and Mr. Loyd have, very wisely as I
think, refrained from committing themselves to any
specific plan for carrying their views of the separation
of functions into effect.   Other writers who have es-
poused the same views have not been so cautious; and
numerous, therefore, have been the schemes which
have been proposed for establishing a single source of
issue, and, for the most part, a government bank.   It
is not my purpose to enter into a detailed examination of any of them; but I cannot help remarking
that, among those which have come under my notice,
the greater part are crude and undigested, while
some of them are so fanciful as to border on the
burlesque.   I have seen none in which the supposed
advantages of the plans sketched out are not greatly
exaggerated; while the inconveniences attending so
great a change are underrated in the same degree,
and in all of them the arguments urged in favour of
the proposed alteration proceed upon a complete misconception of the nature of the machinery, and the
working of the present system, which they seek to
displace.

SUMMARY OF CONCLUSIONS.

The conclusions which I have thus endeavoured to establish are, —

1. That if a purely metallic currency existed in a country situated as this is, transmissions of the precious metals might and would take place occasionally between this and other countries to a considerable amount (five or six millions *at least*), without affecting the amount or value of the currency of the country from which or to which the transmissions were made; and without being a cause or a consequence of alteration in general prices.

2. That consequently the doctrine by which it is maintained that every export or import of bullion in a metallic circulation must entail a corresponding diminution of, or addition to, the quantity of money in circulation, and thus cause a fall or rise of general prices, is essentially incorrect and unsound.

3. That the distinction set up by the currency theory between bank notes and other forms of paper credit, is not founded in any essential difference, except in so far as relates to the lowest denomination of notes, which are required in the transactions between dealers and consumers; that is, in the retail trade, and in the payment of wages.

4. That bills of exchange might, but for the obstacle of stamp duties, be extensively substituted in all transactions of purchase and sale between dealers and dealers for bank notes of 10*l.* and upwards, and that, in point of fact, they were extensively so used until a disproportioned duty was laid upon the smaller bills.

5. That cheques perform the functions of money as conveniently in most respects, as bank notes, and more conveniently in many respects.

6. That bank notes of the higher denominations

are used for peculiar purposes, chiefly in settlements, such as the clearing house, and in sales of landed and fixed property, as regards Bank of England notes; and in the provision markets and cattle fairs, as regards the country circulation; purposes for which substitutes might easily be found if bank notes were suppressed, by bills of exchange, and as regards the settlements among bankers, by exchequer bills, and by what have recently been termed economical expedients.

7. That the amount of bank notes in the hands of the public is determined by the purposes for which they are required, in circulating the capital, and in distributing the revenues of the different orders of the community, valued in gold.

8. That it is not in the power of Banks of Issue, including the Bank of England, to make any direct addition to the amount of notes circulating in their respective districts, however disposed they may be to do so. In the competition of Banks of Issue to get out their notes, there may be an extension of the circulation of some one or more of them in a large district, but it can only be by displacing the notes of rival banks.

9. That neither is it in the power of Banks of Issue *directly* to diminish the total amount of the circulation; particular banks may withhold loans and discounts, and may refuse any longer to issue their own notes; but their notes so withdrawn will be replaced by the notes of other banks, or by other expedients calculated to answer the same purpose.

10. That it is consequently an error to suppose that, however well informed the country bankers might be of the state of the foreign exchanges, and disposed to follow those indications, they would be able to regulate their circulation in conformity with such views. And that it is equally an error to suppose that the Bank of England can exercise a *direct*

power over the exchanges, through the medium of its circulation.

11. That neither the country banks nor the Bank of England have it in their power to make additional issues of their paper, that is, of their notes, come in aid of their banking resources. All advances by way of loan or discount, when the circulation is already full, can only be made by Banks of Issue in the same way as by non-issuing banks, out of their own capital, or that of their depositors.

12. That the prices of commodities do not depend upon the quantity of money indicated by the amount of bank notes, nor upon the amount of the whole of the circulating medium; but that, on the contrary, the amount of the circulating medium is the consequence, of prices.

13. That it is the quantity of money, constituting the revenues of the different orders of the State, under the head of rents, profits, salaries, and wages, destined for current expenditure, that alone forms the limiting principle of the aggregate of money prices, the only prices that can properly come under the designation of general prices. As the cost of production is the limiting principle of supply, so the aggregate of money incomes devoted to expenditure for consumption is the determining and limiting principle of demand.

14. That a reduced rate of interest has no necessary tendency to raise the prices of commodities. On the contrary, it is a cause of diminished cost of production, and consequently of cheapness.*

---

* An objection has been taken to this proposition, as involving with reference to the one immediately following, an apparent inconsistency. It is urged that if a low rate of interest is a cause of cheapness, by parity of reasoning, a high rate of interest must be a cause of dearness: it should seem, therefore, to follow, that the Bank in raising the rate of interest with a view to redress the exchanges would raise the prices of commodities, thus exhibiting the anomaly of advanced prices co-existent

15. That it is only through the rate of interest and the state of credit, that the Bank of England can exercise a direct influence on the foreign exchanges.

16. That the greater or less liability to variation in the rate of interest constitutes, in the next degree only to the preservation of the convertibility of the paper and the solvency of banks, the most important consideration in the regulation of our banking system.

17. That a total separation of the business of issue from that of banking is calculated to produce greater and more abrupt transitions in the rate of interest, and in the state of credit, than the present system of union of the departments.

with an effort on the part of the Bank to restore an influx of bullion. The answer to this objection is, that in the argument leading to the conclusion that a low rate of interest is a cause of cheapness, I have expressly assumed that the reduced rate should be of such duration or permanence as to enter into the cost of production, and the converse holds of a rise in the rate of interest. Now, the operation of the Bank in raising the rate in order to counteract a drain, cannot be considered of such permanence as to affect the cost of production. And the greater the rise in the rate of interest from a forcible operation of the Bank on its securities, the less must be the probability of its duration. But there is a further and still more decisive answer to the objection, and that is, that although the direct operation of the Bank, with the view supposed, is on the rate of interest, it can rarely be effectual, unless the advance be so great, or the circumstances from previous overtrading such as to affect credit and entail failures. Now, commercial discredit, involving extensive failures, is calculated to depress prices, and thus, with an advanced rate of interest, to stop a drain and to force an influx of bullion. And, accordingly, the proposition No. 15, refers to the operation by the Bank on the rate of interest *and the state of credit*, as the only power which it has of directly influencing the exchanges in contradistinction to the power ascribed to it, of acting directly on the amount of the circulation.

POSTSCRIPT.

THERE has recently been a good deal of animation in the markets for colonial produce, attended with a rise in the prices of several articles. And this improvement, and the speculative feeling with which, as usual on such occasions it is accompanied, have been, according to the prevailing doctrine which enters into all the reasonings of brokers in their circulars, and into the accounts furnished to the newspapers, ascribed to *the abundance of money.* Now I would, in the first place, ask those who assign this as the cause of the recent advance of prices to point out a single article in respect of which there are not, in the opinion of persons most conversant with the market, sufficient grounds, by reference to the actual and contingent supply compared with the rate of consumption, to justify a rise of price. A rise, be it observed, from a lower point of depression, in the case of several of the articles, than had ever been known, and in some cases below the lowest cost of production.

During the great and long-continued fall, the dealers both wholesale and retail, and the manufacturers, having been repeatedly disappointed, by finding the price give way after they had got into stock, became disposed to run off their existing stocks before they re-embarked in fresh purchases. From the extensive prevalence of this disposition, there has been, in some of the leading articles of merchandise, a great reduction of stocks, both of raw produce and of finished goods, in the hands of dealers, and manufacturers, and shopkeepers; at the same time, the unprecedently low prices had extended the consumption both at home and abroad. Attention being at length drawn to this state of things, and confidence being acquired that prices had seen their lowest, a general disposition has naturally arisen to get into stock. Now it must be clear that, if a disposition among dealers and manufacturers to get out of stock is attended, as it is known to be, with dull and declining markets, a disposition to replenish their stocks when greatly reduced cannot fail of having an opposite effect. · And as they erred in too confident an anticipation of a further fall of prices, they are liable to err in the opposite direction.

That some rise of prices, under such circumstances, is a necessary result, must be obvious. The degree of the rise must be matter of opinion, in the exercise of which there must be much latitude for miscalculation, till it be brought to the test of facts, viz. the supply and the consumption; the demand by consumers being the ultimate limit to the returns to be received by the wholesale purchasers, whether manufacturers, dealers, or speculators.

If therefore, there be, as there can be no doubt that there is, in every instant of the recent rise of prices, a sufficient, or, at least, a plausible, reason for it on the plain mercantile ground of supply compared with consumption, why call in the aid of abundance of money, meaning the low rate of interest, as a cause originating or even contributing? · And why, if the low rate of interest is the present *stimulus* to purchases, did it not *stimulate* dealers and speculators a twelvemonth ago, when the rate of interest was as low as it is now, or only six months ago, when there was not a trace of a speculative tendency in the markets for commodities? or why, above all, did it not operate in deterring the dealers and manufacturers from getting out of stock, and in thus arresting the decline of prices which (with the exception of those of corn) took place nearly, *pari passu*, with the fall in the rate of interest, or as it would in the modern use of the word be called, the increasing abundance of money from 1840 to the summer of 1843 ?

I have just now before me some of the circulars of the most considerable brokers in the markets for colonial produce; for it is in these that the recent advance of prices has given occasion to the supposition that what is called the abundance of money has been the cause of the rise. And it is not a little amusing to observe, that while the writers of the circulars think it incumbent upon them, according to the prevailing fashion, to ascribe considerable influence to the abundance of money, the information which they convey, respecting each of the articles that has been the subject of advance, is quite decisive in proving that the recent rise of prices has nothing to do with the low rate of interest, but is in each instance *amply justified upon the simple and obvious ground of a diminution of supply and an increase of the consumption.*

So striking and whimsical is this exhibition of the prevalence of what may be called *currency pedantry*, that although a detailed reference to actual or comparative prices, and the state of markets, formed no part of my plan in this publication, I am induced to give the following brief view of them, as showing how little they bear out the opinion expressed in the circulars, that it is the abundance of unemployed capital that has led to the investments in commodities.

In a circular dated 2d March, 1844, full of just and accurate information of the position of the markets for transatlantic produce, the details relative to that position are prefaced by the following remarks : —

" A very large amount of capital, both here and on the Continent, has been employed in the purchase of goods, and almost every article in the Colonial market has already felt the influence of it. *These operations have not altogether been influenced by any calculation of supply and demand, but were entered into from a conviction that the lowest point of depression had been reached, and.that the abundance of unemployed money and the improved condition of trade were at length about to cause a general advance in prices.* This effect has been partially attained; during the past fortnight an increased value of from ten to fifteen per cent. has been realised upon coffee, sugar, rice, and many minor articles, and more animation has been witnessed in Mincing Lane than has existed for the last ten years.

"It cannot be denied that a decided movement has commenced, and that, from many circumstances, it bears the probability of further extension. The great commercial difficulties under which nations have laboured have been mainly surmounted;—the financial condition of Great Britain has been materially improved,—money is still very abundant, and the Bank coffers are full of bullion. All public funds have increased in value, and investments in railway securities (from their magnitude a most important item) have become less eligible, owing to their advanced price. *It was therefore almost an inevitable consequence, that articles of foreign merchandise which bore so depressed a value should attract money to them; and if the operations are confined within reasonable bounds, they seem legitimate enough, but it will become important to keep a watchful eye on the money market.*"

In former times, and in plain mercantile language, the expression of the first sentence would have been simply, that large purchases had been made, and that prices had risen in consequence—a very natural consequence. But the passage following, which I have marked with italics, exemplifies, in a pre-eminent degree, the tendency to introduce the money market, *à tort et à travers*, into the markets for commodities. If the operations alluded to were not altogether influenced by a calculation of supply and demand, all that could be said of them would be, that they were very silly ones. But it will be seen by the showing of this very circular, that they were very wise ones, proceeding as they are proved to have done, upon a very sound and rational view of supply and demand. Before entering upon the proofs to that effect, I would merely call attention to the last sentence of the above extract, remarking, however, upon it only, that instead of recommending to the operators in the markets for commodities to keep a watchful eye on the money market, the sounder recommendation would be to shut their eyes altogether to it, but to be wide awake to all circumstances affecting the actual and probable supply on the one hand, and the consumption, whether at home or abroad, on the other.

The articles alluded to in the circular as having experienced the most decided improvement are, sugar, coffee, and rice, and the following are the statements respecting these descriptions of produce : —

" *Sugar.*—There has been a very steady demand for British Plantation sugar throughout the month, and the West India market continuing very barely supplied, especially with good and fine qualities, and the arrivals of East India and Mauritius being very moderate, prices have advanced 1*s.* @ 2*s.*, the greatest. rise being on the lower descriptions. An additional reason for this improvement is the large increase of the deliveries for the first two months of this year, which not only exceed the same period both of 1842 and 1843, but are in excess of the imports to this date, by nearly 13,000 tons, thus producing a large decrease of stock ; to this circumstance may also be added a general belief that the crop in Jamaica will be deficient. The supplies near at hand are not large, prices consequently, are likely to be well maintained, particularly as consumption is evidently so largely on the increase.

" The Imports of *East* and *West India* and *Mauritius* into Great Britain amounted to 19,000 tons, against 26,500 in 1843, and 19,900 in 1842 ; the deliveries to 30,800 tons, against 26,800 in 1843, and 21,000 in 1842 ; and the stock to 29,800 tons, against 39,500 in 1843, and 28,800 in 1842."

And the demand for foreign sugars, independent of short stocks relatively to the exports, was increased by a prevailing impression of the chance of a reduction of duty.

" *Coffee.* — The business in the home market has been very large, the trade having bought extensively. The imports have fallen off, and the consumption has again increased, and as there cannot be any arrivals of importance for some time, there is a probability of still further advance in price, as the rise in the value of foreign descriptions suitable for the home trade will prevent their being brought into competition. Nearly 13,000 bags of *Ceylon* have changed hands, at 65*s.* @ 68*s.* 6*d.*, which is an advance of 2*s.* @ 3*s.* since the first ultimo. In foreign *East India* sorts 3,000 bags of *Java* have been sold at 36*s.* @ 53*s.*; from 3,000 @ 4,000 bags *Padang* at 26*s.* @ 32*s.*; and 1,500 bales *Mocha*, at 68*s.* @ 75*s.*

" A very important speculation has taken place in all descriptions of foreign coffee. It commenced in Holland, and has been extended to London, Hamburgh and Antwerp, and will doubtless spread throughout Europe. Statements of an extensive operation were privately put forth in certain quarters as early as the month of November last, and measures were silently prepared which have since been effectually accomplished. Upwards of 300,000 bags (19,000 tons) have been sold here and on the Continent, and an advance of 3*s.* @ 5*s.* has been realized in this market. These large transactions appeared rather unexpectedly, for although the stocks at the end of the year were less than it was calculated they would be, coffee had been so long subjected to neglect, that it was not a favourite article."

Could there be a better ground for a rise of price than that the stocks were less than had been calculated, and that the article had been long neglected? There seems, likewise, to have been an idea prevalent that some alteration of the duty might take place.

" *Rice.* — In common with many articles of extensive general consumption, rice of late has attracted attention as an object for investment, and large transactions accordingly have resulted therefrom, causing an advance in prices of 1*s.* @ 1*s.* 6*d.* ℔ cwt. The quotations for *Bengal* being now 12*s.* @

12*s.* 6*d.* ℔ cwt., and *Java* 9*s.* @ 12*s.* No less than 50,000 bags have changed hands in the course of the month, and the market still presents a buoyant aspect. The imports for the first two months amount to 11,300 bags, against 27,200 for the corresponding period in 1843, and the stock stands at 107,000 bags, against 139,600."

The speculation in cotton, and the rapid rise in the price of that article, took place some months ago, when reports of a deficiency of the crop of 1843 began to gain ground. That the crop has been a deficient one is on all hands now admitted; but as the advance of price had some weeks since reached the utmost height, which, as the result of the conflict of opinions and interests, the deficiency of the crop, combined with a view to the rate of consumption, seemed to warrant, this article has not participated in the animation which is described as prevailing in the markets for several other articles of transatlantic produce.

It would weary the reader to go on with a statement respecting other articles which had risen in price. Suffice it to say that there is not one, as to which it is not proved, that, upon the principle of supply and demand, there has been clearly a ground for some advance, and in no one does the rise of price hitherto appear to have been unreasonable.

While Indigo, of which the crop is reported to be unusually large, has of late experienced a fall of upwards of 20 per cent.

At the same time, several important articles, such, among others, as those of Baltic produce, are in a perfectly quiescent state.

I will only further give an extract from another price current, dated 5th March, 1844, for the purpose of a remark which I shall have to make upon it.

We confess it was always matter of surprise to us to see coffee so long and so fearfully depressed, not being like many

K 2

things which are deteriorated by keeping ; this, on the contrary, improves. *The abundance of money having at length caused the attention of capitalists to be turned to goods,* coffee has been one of the favoured articles ; *the speculation commenced abroad,* but its influence was soon communicated to our market, causing, as before noticed, a rapid and great advance. The bulk of the transactions here have comprised Brazil and St. Domingo. The impression of many is that prices will be forced up still higher ; and this is more likely to be the case, if, as is stated, the small merchants and shopkeepers abroad are entirely bare of stock.

Here, again, we have the money market gratuitously brought in. It was not the abundance of money that directed the attention of the *capitalists* (as it is becoming the fashion to call wealthy merchants), but the low price and long previous neglect of the article. But what I have principally to remark upon is, the observation in the above extract, — that the small merchants and shopkeepers abroad had become bare of stock. This process of getting out of stock by the dealers commonly accompanies, and is both cause and effect of declining prices when supplies have increased or consumption fallen off for some length of time, beyond the expectation of the dealers; till stocks have diminished, and consumption has increased, when attention is drawn to them, and a re-action is the consequence.

The best informed merchants and dealers are commonly the first to have their attention so drawn ; and, as in the case of the large coffee speculation, which has had its origin in Holland, the parties to it having the most extensive correspondence on the Continent, were the best calculated and most likely to obtain information, and to act successfully upon it, respecting an article, the supplies of which are derived from many sources, and the stocks and consumers of which are spread over the whole civilised world.

They have thus anticipated the smaller merchants and dealers, as is mentioned in the circular. It is not their abundance of capital that directed their attention, for of capital they have long had abundance, but their attention being habitually engaged in the article, they must have been collecting information respecting it for some time, till they became assured that the consumption at the existing prices, which were below the cost of production, was rapidly gaining ground upon the supply ; and when they became so assured, they acted upon that view, as they would equally have done, whether the interest of money had been 2 per cent. or 5 per cent. The only difference that this makes is, that, in a small degree, they may be induced to realise by re-sale at a lower price than if the cost had been somewhat raised by the charge of higher interest.

I have been induced to notice this point at some length, because I am convinced that opinions like those contained in the extracts which I have quoted are calculated to mislead, by inducing, in those to whom they are an authority, a reliance upon a supposed general cause, which has no existence, to the neglect of the more correct rule of reasoning and acting, according to the best information as to the actual and contingent supply and the rate of consumption. It cannot be too often repeated, that abundance of money in the hands of capitalists is in itself a cause of cheapness, while abundance of money in the hands of consumers is a cause of dearness.

There is one other remark suggested by the accounts in the Circulars, of the animation which prevails in Mincing Lane, and that is, that the speculation which has attracted most attention, namely, that in coffee has had its rise in Holland, and has extended in its effects to other towns on the Continent, as well as to this country ; the prices abroad, however, being full as high as *here*, or, if anything, higher. And I understand that, in the case of nearly all the articles which have recently experienced a considerable advance in this country, the advance on the Continent of Europe is in fully the same, if not in a greater proportion. And, generally speaking, prices on the Continent, I mean of articles of consumption of its population, are fully as high in proportion as they are here, bating corn and such other articles as are subject to high or prohibitory duties in this country. Now, according to the currency theory, prices abroad ought to be depressed, and at a much lower range than they are here, seeing the large quantity of the precious metals which has been abstracted from them to form the accumulation of bullion now existing in the coffers of the Bank of England.

The present state of facts, therefore, may be considered as adding, if any addition were wanting, to the arguments which have in the foregoing pages been adduced to show the unsoundness of that theory.

May 15. 1844.

The markets for produce have ever since the preceding pages were written been in a perfectly sound and unexcited state, notwithstanding the continued abundance of money ; that is, as low a rate of interest as ever.

APPENDIX.

(A.) Page 68.

FROM a wish not to encumber the argument as stated in the text, to which this is a note, I then abstained from noticing a prepossession or prejudice (besides that of the assumed analogy of a compulsory government paper), which, in the popular view, leads irresistibly to the persuasion, that the quantity of money, according to whatever may be the supposed test of the quantity, must have a direct influence on the prices of commodities. The prepossession or prejudice to which I allude, has its rise in the following very specious reasoning.

The prices of commodities depend upon supply and demand; now, *given* the supply, prices depend upon the demand. But money is the instrument of demand; therefore, any increase of money must be an increase of demand, and must consequently raise prices; and as bank notes are by the definition money, an increase of bank notes must increase the demand for, and raise the prices of commodities.

The following passage of the late Mr. James Mill's Essay on Political Economy (3d ed. p. 131.) is calculated to countenance this, which, as expressed in these general terms, I cannot but consider as an erroneous view : —

" It is not difficult to perceive that it is the total amount of
" the money in any country, which determines what portion
" of that quantity shall exchange for a certain portion of the
" goods or commodities of that country.

" If we suppose that all the goods of this country are on one
" side, all the money on the other, and that they are exchanged
" at once against one another, it is obvious that one tenth, or
" one hundredth, or any other part of the goods, will exchange
" against one tenth or any other part of the whole of the money
" and that this tenth &c., will be a great quantity or small
" exactly in proportion as the whole quantity of the money of
" the country is great or small. If this were the state of the
" facts, therefore, it is evident that the value would depend
" wholly upon the quantity of it. It will appear that the
" case is precisely the same in the actual state of the facts."

K 4

Mr. Senior, in one of his lectures on the value of money, and in the article of the Edinburgh Review, which I have before referred to, has commented on the above passage in Mr. Mill's essay, and pointed out the fallacy of it, in overlooking the consideration, that it is the cost of production of the precious metals, and not their quantity, which constitutes their value, and determines the prices of commodities with reference to the cost of production of the latter measured in metallic value.

Mr. Mill, however, in a subsequent passage, page 167, illustrates his view by a hypothetical case. " Suppose," he says, " the market to be a very narrow one, of bread solely on " the one side and money on the other. Suppose that the or- " dinary state of the market is one hundred loaves on the one " side, and one hundred shillings on the other, the price of bread " accordingly a shilling a loaf. Suppose, in these circumstances, " that the quantity of loaves is increased to two hundred, while " the money remains the same ; it is obvious that the price of " the bread must fall one half, or to sixpence per loaf."

It should seem from this last passage that Mr. Mill had so far qualified, or perhaps, more strictly speaking, lost sight of the view conveyed by the former passage, as to confine the supposition of the quantity of money affecting prices, to that which was in the pockets or hands of the consumers, going to market to supply their immediate wants. And to this limited extent it may be admitted that the quantity of money has an influence on prices. But, so limited, this proposition has nothing in common with the doctrine of the currency theory, which ascribes an influence to the quantity of money indicated by the amount of bank notes in circulation, or by the whole of the circulating medium.

(B.) Page 79.

The expression in the text respecting the power of purchase by persons having capital and credit may require some explanation, which I have here accordingly to give, accompanied by an illustration of my meaning by reference to actual occurrences. What I mean to say is, that a person having the reputation of capital enough for his regular business, and enjoying good credit in his trade, if he takes a sanguine view of the prospect of a rise of price of the article in which he deals, and is favoured by circumstances in the outset and progress of his speculation, may effect purchases to an extent perfectly enormous compared with his capital. The conditions requisite are that the market should be a large one, and the article susceptible of great fluctuation of price, from political or physical causes ; and, in fact, it is only articles of this description that are the subject of speculations sufficiently extensive to attract notice. I propose to exemplify this by what occurred in the Tea trade in 1839, when the disturbances in China broke out; and by the speculation in the Corn trade between 1838 and 1842.

Among the earliest speculations for an advance in the price of Tea, in consequence of our dispute with China in 1839, were several retail grocers and tea dealers. There was a general disposition among the trade to get into stock, that is, to lay in at once a quantity which would meet the probable demand from their customers for several months to come. Some, however, among them, more sanguine and adventurous than the rest, availed themselves of their credit with the importers and wholesale dealers for purchasing quantities much beyond the estimated demand in their own business. As the purchases were made in the first instance ostensibly, and perhaps really, for the legitimate purposes, and within the limits of their regular business, the parties were enabled to buy without the condition of any deposit; whereas speculators, known to be such, are required to pay 2l. per chest, to cover any probable difference of price which might arise before the expiration of the prompt, which, for this article, is three months. *Without, therefore, the outlay of a single farthing of actual capital or currency in any shape*, they made purchases to a considerable extent; and, with the profit realised on the resale of a part of these purchases, they were enabled to pay the deposit on further quantities when required, as was the case when the extent of the purchases attracted attention.

In this way, the speculation went on at advancing prices (100 per cent. and upwards), till nearly the expiration of the prompt: and if at that time circumstances had been such as to justify the apprehension, which at one time prevailed, that all future supplies would be cut off, the prices might have still further advanced, and, at any rate, not have retrograded. In this case, the speculators might have realised by sales, if not all the profit they had anticipated, a very handsome sum, upon which they might have been enabled to extend their business greatly, or to retire from it altogether, with a reputation for great sagacity in thus making their fortune. But instead of this favourable result, it so happened that two or three cargoes of Tea which had been transhipped were admitted, contrary to expectation, to entry on their arrival here, and it was found that further indirect shipments were in progress. Thus the supply was increased beyond the calculation of the speculators; and, at the same time, the consumption had been diminished by the high price. There was, consequently, a violent reaction on the market: the speculators were unable to sell without such a sacrifice as disabled them from fulfilling their engagements, and several of them consequently failed. Among these, one was mentioned who, having a capital not exceeding 1200*l.*, which was locked up in his business, had contrived to buy 4000 chests, value above 80,000*l.*, the loss upon which was about 16,000*l.*

The other example which I have to give is that of the operation on the corn market between 1838 and 1842. There was an instance of a person who, when he entered on his extensive speculations, was, as it appeared by the subsequent examination of his affairs, possessed of a capital not exceeding 5000*l.*, but, being successful in the outset, and favoured by circumstances in the progress of his operations, he contrived to make purchases to such an extent, that when he stopped payment his engagements were found to amount to between 500,000*l.* and 600,000*l.* Other instances might be cited of parties without any capital at all, who, by dint of mere credit, were enabled, while the aspect of the market favoured their views, to make purchases to a very great extent.

And be it observed, that these speculations involving enormous purchases, on little or no capital, were carried on in 1839 and 1840, when the money market was in its most contracted state; or when, according to modern phraseology, there was the greatest scarcity of money.

(C.) Page 84.

It is not easy to imagine a view less reconcilable with a correct appreciation of the state of things as regards prices, in connection with the state of the circulation in 1839, than is contained in the following question and answer in the examination of Mr. Norman by the Committee on Banks of Issue, the material fact being admitted, *that prices were firmly maintained at that time, notwithstanding an advance in the rate of interest to* 6 *per cent.* : —

" 1926. *Chairman.* — Were not, generally, the prices of " commodities in 1839 maintained during that period *by*

" *those issues of the Bank*, in defiance of their rule? *Ans.* I
" believe that prices were very firmly maintained during
" 1839; but I believe also that the restrictive measures of
" the Bank *had an effect upon prices;* because I am confident
" that the exportation of the precious metals was by no
" means equal to the demand for extra-foreign payment; and
" in explanation I would say that I apprehend the foreign
" payment for corn from the autumn of 1838 to have been
" fully ten millions sterling, and I cannot trace an export-
" ation exceeding about six or seven millions."

The version in the answer of Mr. Palmer to the question,
subjoined, conveys, as it strikes me, the correct view : —

" 1473. *Chairman.* — If more stringent measures for the
" purpose of reducing the accommodation to the commerce
" of this country had been taken (in 1839), would not prices
" necessarily have come down, and exports thus have been
" increased for the purpose of meeting the foreign payment?
" *Ans.* I think it is very doubtful, from the extent and power
" of capital in this country, and the diminished stocks of
" goods then in the possession of the merchants, whether
" that result could have been attained."

(D.) Page 112.

Paper communicated by Mr. Pennington.

" It has been proposed that the business of the Bank shall
" be separated into two distinct departments, one to be
" called the circulation department, the other the deposit de-
" partment; that the circulating department shall hold a
" fixed and unvarying amount of securities, and that its func-
" tions shall be confined solely to the exchange of gold for
" notes, and of notes for gold ; and that the deposit depart-
" ment shall manage the funds intrusted to it on the ordinary
" principles which are observed by the London bankers, and
" independently of the promissory note department.

" It may be worth while to inquire, what would be the
" probable operation of such a plan.

" In carrying it into execution, I apprehend, it would be
" proper, in the first instance, to assign to the deposit depart-
" ment such a proportion of the securities, and of the bullion,
" in possession of the Bank, as would, together, be equal to
" the amount of the deposits. Thus, if the Bank held eighteen
" millions of securities, and nine millions of bullion, against
" eighteen millions of outstanding notes, and nine millions of
" deposits, it would probably be deemed expedient to assign

" to the deposit department six millions of securities, and
" three millions of bullion, and to retain in the circulating
" department six millions of bullion, and twelve millions of
" securities.

" If such a separation were made, it is obvious, that as the
" exchange of gold for notes, or of notes for gold, between
" the two branches, *would not affect the amount of bank paper*
" *in the hands of the public,* and as such interchange might
" take place frequently, and to a great extent, *the increase or*
" *diminution of outstanding notes would form no certain criterion*
" *of the amount of paper circulating out of doors,* unless it
" were, at the same time, known what amount of notes was
" held by the department of deposit.

" Disregarding, for the present, any objection which it
" may be supposed would arise from this consideration, let
" us at once proceed to inquire what effect would be produced
" by a demand upon the Bank for bullion.

" The action and condition of the deposit department will
" be more distinctly perceived, if we suppose that, under cir-
" cumstances above stated, the whole of the three millions of
" bullion are exchanged, on its first establishment, for three
" millions of notes. The position of the two departments
" would then be as follows : —

" Circulating Department.		Deposit Department.	
" Outstanding notes	- £21,000,000	Deposits - -	£9,000,000
" Securities - - -	£12,000,000	Securities - -	£6,000,000
" Bullion - - -	9,000,000	Bank notes - -	3,000,000

" This being the position of the two departments, let us
" suppose that an adverse foreign exchange has created a
" demand upon the Bank for bullion for exportation. Now,
" such a demand for bullion may be satisfied, either by a
" reduction of the notes in the hands of the public, or by a
" reduction of the deposits at the Bank. If the former, then
" the separation of the business of the Bank into two depart-
" ments will have answered the purpose expected from it; if
" the latter, then, in so far as relates to the increase or dimi-
" nution of Bank notes in the hands of the public, by the
" action of the foreign exchange, no satisfactory result will
" have been produced. In the latter case, no advantage in
" the regulation of the circulation will have resulted from the
" separation.

" It may, perhaps, be said, that if the business of banking
" were separated from that of circulation, and conducted in
" the manner and upon the principles which are adopted by

" the private bankers of the metropolis, a diminution of de-
" posits would be immediately followed by the sale or realiza-
" tion of a corresponding amount of securities, and thus the
" amount of bank notes, in the external circulation, would
" be reduced to an extent commensurate with the delivery of
" bullion.

" But such a sale or realization of securities, in similar
" circumstances, may be effected under the present system of
" management. Whether the existing system be continued,
" or the business of the Bank be separated into two depart-
" ments, the sale or realization of securities must depend on
" the views and the discretion of the directors of the Bank.
" The only difference between the two cases is this; that the
" counteracting effect occasioned by paying out bank notes to
" the depositors would be limited to three millions: upon the
" present system it may be carried to a much greater extent.

" It may be observed, moreover, that if the demand for
" bullion for exportation should exceed three millions, and if
" that demand should fall on the deposit department, that
" department would be reduced to the necessity, *either of*
" *forcibly realizing a portion of its securities, or of stopping*
" *payment at a time when the circulating department was*
" *abundantly provided with specie.*

" It may be desirable to apply the foregoing principles and
" observations to the actual position of the Bank, at certain
" periods, within the last four years.

" In January 1834 the liabilities and assets were as fol-
" lows:

" Circulation	-	-	£18,236,000	Securities	-	-	£23,596,000
" Deposits	-	-	13,101,000	Bullion	-	-	9,948,000
" Rest	-	-	2,207,000				£33,544,000
			£33,544,000				

" If, at that time, it had been determined to divide the
" business of the Bank into two departments, it would
" probably have been deemed expedient to assign 12,000,000*l.*
" of the securities to the circulating department, as a fixed
" amount which was at no future time to be exceeded. The
" remaining securities would, of course, go to the bank-
" ing department. The outstanding notes, amounting to
" 18,236,000*l.*, would then have for their basis 12,000,000*l.*
" of securities, and 6,236,000*l.* of bullion. But, as the de-
" posit department would probably prefer notes to gold, on
" account of the greater convenience of the former, the posi-
" tion of the two departments would have been as follows:—

CIRCULATING DEPARTMENT.

	Circulation	Securities	Bullion
Notes in the hands of the public - -	18,236		
Notes in the banking department - -	3,712		
	21,948	12,000	9,948

BANKING DEPARTMENT.

	Deposits	Securities	Bank Notes
Deposits - -	13,101	—	—
Rest - -	2,207	11,596	3,712
	15,308		

The following would have been the position of two branches at the under-mentioned periods:

Date	Notes	Amount	Circulation	Securities	Bullion		Amount	Deposits	Securities	Bank Notes
1834: Dec.	Notes: Public - -	18,304	18,720	12,000	6,720	Deposits -	12,256	15,778	14,362	416
	Banking department -	416				Rest -	2,532			
1835: July.	Notes: Public - -	18,283	18,283	12,000	6,283	Deposits -	11,561	14,205	14,244	nil.
	Banking department -	nil.				Rest -	2,644			
1836: Jan.	Notes: Public - -	17,262	19,076	12,000	7,076	Deposits -	19,169	21,768	19,954	1,814
	Banking department -	1,814				Rest -	2,599			
Aug.	Notes: Public - -	18,061	18,325	12,000	6,325	Deposits -	14,796	17,609	17,345	264
	Banking department -	264				Rest -	2,813			
1838: Jan.	Notes: Public - -	17,900	20,895	12,000	8,895	Deposits -	10,992	13,601	10,606	2,995
	Banking department -	2,995				Rest -	2,609			
1839: Jan.	Notes: Public - -	18,201	21,336	12,000	9,336	Deposits -	10,315	12,815	9,680	3,135
	Banking department -	3,135				Rest -	2,500			
July.	Notes: Public - -	18,049	18,049	12,000	3,785	Deposits -	7,955	10,641	12,905	nil.
	Banking department -	nil.				Rest -	2,686			

" It will be seen, by the foregoing statement, that if the
" business of the Bank had been separated into two depart-
" ments in January 1834, and if the rule, which we have
" supposed to have been at that time established, had, since,
" been inflexibly adhered to, the paper issues of the circu-
" lating department in July last (1839) would have been
" less by 2,364,000*l*. than their actual amount at that period,
" and the cash of the deposit department would have been
" wholly exhausted. In July 1835 and July 1839 the secu-
" rities held by the deposit department would have exceeded
" the aggregate amount of the rest and the deposits. This
" excess of securities over deposits this department could not
" have held, unless the circulating department had transgressed
" the prescribed rule to an extent equal to the amount of that
" excess.

" In order to prevent the exhaustion of its cash, the bank-
" ing department would, no doubt, have endeavoured to
" withdraw bank notes from the hands of the public, by dis-
" posing of a large amount of its securities. A rigid adherence
" to the rule by the directors of the circulating department,
" and a due regard to its safety by the managers of the bank-
" ing branch, would have rendered the amount of the securities
" in possession of the latter, in July last, less by three or four
" millions than it appears actually to have been ; or, which
" comes to the same thing, the amount of bank notes in the
" hands of the public at that time would have been three or
" four millions less than it appears to have actually been.
" *The consequence would have been, a very severe pressure on*
" *the money market.*

" Hitherto, we have supposed the business of the Bank to
" be separated into two distinct departments, and a formal
" apportionment of debts and assets to have been made. Now
" without such a formal separation and apportionment, pre-
" cisely the same action upon the currency would result from
" the strict observance of the following rule ; namely, that
" the Bank shall not, upon any occasion, issue bank notes be-
" yond a certain amount (that amount we have supposed to
" be 12,000,000*l*.), except upon the deposit of bullion. If
" this rule had been adopted in January 1839, and afterwards
" rigidly adhered to, *a great reduction of the securities held*
" *by the Bank would have been necessary, in order to avoid*
" *a suspension of the payment of its deposits.* It is probable,
" indeed, that such a reduction of the securities would have
" arrested the drain of treasure at an early period of the year.
" If, however, the drain had continued, notwithstanding the

" reduction, it would have been necessary, in July last (1839),
" to have carried the reduction to the extent of three or four
" millions below the amount which the Bank actually held at
" that period.

" Whether a formal separation of the Bank into two depart-
" ments take place, or the rule last mentioned be adopted, it
" may be expected that *the public will be exposed to very*
" *great alternations of comparative ease and difficulty in the*
" *operations of the money market.*

" It may here be proper to observe, that the difference be-
" tween the rule above mentioned and that explained by
" Mr. Horsley Palmer and Mr. Norman in their evidence is
" this ; — that, while the former rule would preclude the
" Bank from issuing notes in the payment of deposits to a
" greater extent than is equal, in amount, to the difference
" between the amount of notes at any time outstanding and
" 12,000,000*l.*, plus the amount of bullion in possession of the
" Bank, the latter would allow the Bank to substitute notes
" for deposits to an unlimited extent.   The former rule would
" be the same in its operation as a division of the Bank into
" two departments.   The sole effect of the latter would be,
" the increase or diminution of the aggregate amount of the
" notes and deposits of the Bank with the increase or dimi-
" nution of its bullion.

" There is one point connected with the proposed division
" of the Bank into two departments to which I have not
" adverted, but which it may be material to notice.   It has
" been suggested, that, in order to increase the disposable
" funds of the banking department, it would be desirable
" that a certain portion of the capital of the Bank, now lent
" to the state, should be made available for banking pur-
" poses.   By this I apprehend it is meant, that a portion of
" the 3 per cent. stock in which the original capital of the
" Bank is invested shall be sold, and the proceeds of the
" sale invested in other securities, and in commercial loans
" and discounts, at the pleasure and discretion of the Bank.

" Of this suggestion it may be observed, that it is a pro-
" posal to withdraw a certain amount of funds from the use
" and employment of one class of persons, in order that it
" may be transferred by the Bank to the use and employment
" of another class of persons.   By this process no new funds
" would be created in the money market.   The change
" would be merely the transfer of funds already existing
" from one kind of investment to another.   The operation
" would be the same as that of an individual stockholder

" who sells his stock in order to employ the money arising
" from the sale in commercial discounts. The operation
" of the individual stockholder would, in its consequences,
" be comparatively of little importance ; but if five millions
" of the original capital of the Bank were sold, as has been
" proposed, and the proceeds of the sale mixed up with and
" employed in the same manner as the deposits at the Bank,
" although no greater reserve of bank notes in the banking
" department, in consequence of this accession of funds,
" would be necessary, yet the varying employment of funds
" of such magnitude, during alternate periods of commercial
" excitement and depression, might produce a prodigious
" effect upon the general circulation. At one time the
" additional fund might be employed in commercial loans
" and discounts; at another time a great part of it might be
" withdrawn from the public, and held by the Bank, in bank
" notes and specie; thus creating an alternate abundance
" and scarcity of money in the hands of the public, at the
" pleasure of the Bank."

Thus far was communicated to me in the paper by Mr.
Pennington, and I have now to add the following extract
from his letter to Mr. K. Finlay : —

" If it should be determined to adopt the proposed plan of
" separation, the most difficult, and by far the most im-
" portant, point for consideration, would be, to determine
" the fixed amount of securities to be held by the department
" of issue. If that point were once properly settled, the
" principal object of the plan might be attained, without a
" formal division into two departments of the business of the
" Bank. Such a separation would be desirable only as it
" might afford a better security than could be otherwise
" obtained, that the fixed amount of securities would, at no
" future time, nor upon any occasion, however urgent, be
" exceeded.

" In the supposed case above stated, namely, that previous
" to the separation, the Bank is in possession of 18,000,000l.
" of securities, and 9,000,000l. of treasure, against 18,000,000l.
" of outstanding notes, and 9,000,000l. of deposits, I have
" assumed the fixed amount of securities, to be held by the
" department of issue, to be 12,000,000l. If that were the
" amount fixed, the outstanding notes must, according to the
" prescribed rule, be 21,000,000l., of which, as 18,000,000l.
" are supposed to be in the hands of the public, 3,000,000l.
" must necessarily be placed at the disposal of the banking
" department.

"In a letter to Mr. Tooke, lately published, Colonel
" Torrens has assumed, for the purpose of illustration, the
" same supposed case, and has fixed the amount of securities
" to be held by the circulating department, at 9,000,000l.
" In so fixing the amount, he places (under the circumstances
" supposed) the banking department precisely in the situ-
" ation, the possibility of which is contemplated by Mr.
" Tooke, that is, that of being without either notes or gold
" wherewith to pay any immediate demands of the de-
" positors, and of being obliged, in order to obtain the
" requisite means, to force on the money market the sale of
" a portion of its securities. He supposes that, for this
" purpose, a sale of 3,000,000l. of securities would be neces-
" sary, and that, consequently, the 18,000,000l. previously
" in the hands of the public, would be reduced to 15,000,000l.

" Notwithstanding this pressure on the money market, we
" are to suppose that an adverse exchange has produced a
" demand upon the Bank for gold to the extent of 3,000,000l.
" Colonel Torrens then says, ' The 3,000,000l. bank notes,
" held by the deposit department as reserve, would be drawn
" out by the depositors, and paid into the circulating depart-
" ment in exchange for gold; while the directors of the
" deposit department, in order to recover a reserve equal
" to one-third of their deposits, would be obliged to sell
" 2,000,000l. of the 6,000,000l. held in securities. The
" results would be, that in the circulating department, the
" bullion would be reduced from 9,000,000l. to 6,000,000l.,
" and the circulation from 18,000,000l. to 15,000,000l.; and
" that in the deposit department, the deposits would be re-
" duced from 9,000,000l. to 6,000,000l.; the securities from
" 6,000,000l. to 4,000,000l. ; and the reserve from 3,000,000l.
" to 2,000,000l. It is self-evident that the effect would be,
" not only a contraction of the circulation, but a limitation
" of the power to overtrade in discounts and loans.'
" To reduce the amount of bank notes in the hands of the
" public from 18,000,000l. to 13,000,000l., *would*, indeed,
" *effectually prevent overtrading in discounts and loans.*
" Although so extreme a case as that put by Colonel
" Torrens is not likely to occur, yet if it were to occur, all
" the consequences which he has described would ensue,
" without a separation of debts and assets, from a strict
" observance of the rule described in the paper communicated
" to Mr. Tooke, namely, that the Bank shall not, upon any
" occasion, issue notes beyond a certain fixed amount, except
" upon receiving into its possession a corresponding amount

" of gold. A division of the business of the Bank into two
" departments, or a strict observance of the rule, without the
" division, would produce the same results.

" There is one material circumstance, however, which
" renders it doubtful whether a separation of functions in the
" way proposed, would be the most effectual means of ob-
" taining the requisite security for the due observance of the
" rule.

" Hitherto it has been the practice of the Bank of England
" to cancel all notes brought in for payment, — never to
" re-issue them. Now, although an adherence to this practice
" would not occasion any insuperable difficulty in carrying
" out the proposed arrangement, yet it would render it
" necessary that the banking department should generally
" keep on hand a very large amount of gold, or of notes
" signed, and ready for delivery. To hold a very large
" amount of notes signed and completely executed, might be
" deemed hazardous or inconvenient. If, in order to avoid
" that risk and inconvenience, the banking department were
" to keep on hand the cancelled notes, and require from the
" department of issue new notes for the old ones, at such
" times, and to such an extent, as suited its occasional wants
" and convenience, the department of issue would be virtually
" a depository for the banking department, and, through the
" banking department, a depository, to a greater or less
" extent, for others. Arrangements might, no doubt, be
" made, and a system of checks contrived, that would prevent
" any violation of the principle of the plan ; *but the requisite*
" *machinery would be a matter of considerable nicety, of which*
" *the operation and the object would not easily be perceived and*
" *understood by the public.*"

SUPPLEMENTARY CHAPTER.

ON THE MEASURES BEFORE PARLIAMENT FOR THE RE-
NEWAL OF THE BANK CHARTER, AND THE REGULATION
OF BANKS IN ENGLAND AND WALES.

THE publication of a second edition of this Pamphlet allows me the opportunity of adding a few remarks on the pending measures relative to banking.

The views of government, in reference to the regulations of banking in England, are now before the Public.

The measures proposed in pursuance of that policy are embodied in eleven resolutions, which were submitted by the Government to the House of Commons on the 6th instant (May), and will be the subject of debate in Parliament.

The policy in pursuance of which those measures are proposed, was developed in a speech of some length by Sir Robert Peel. The merits of that speech have been characterised in a manner perfectly accordant with my estimate of them in a leading article of the *Times;* and as, agreeing in the view thus taken, I should fail of conveying it in language of my own so characteristically clear and appropriate as that in which it is there expressed, I am induced to give the following extract, premising that in the part immediately preceding, the proposed arrangements are spoken of as meeting with general approbation, in which the writer of the article concurs.

" Sir R. Peel's speech was, we think, scarcely so good as his propositions. His premises were excellent ; his conclusions admirable: all that was wanting was a connection between the two. The speech failed precisely in that which he professed, with some parade to have accomplished. It failed in developing clearly the principles on which the proposed changes were based. It had a beginning and ending, but seemed to have lost its middle in the delivery. He laid his foundations deep and palpable in the gold mines of Mexico; his towering results are those which have long furnished a landmark to the sagacious speculator on agios and exchanges; but there was a large intervening space of impenetrable and unmeaning cloud, displaying no visible or intelligible form to any imaginations but those which have already mastered the intricate and perilous ground which lies beneath. Sir Robert Peel expends much time in a true, ingenious, and very complete demolition of the Birmingham financiers. One-third part of his speech is occupied in showing that gold the money of this country is, and that gold it ought to remain — an exposition which, however valuable in itself, might, we think, without any serious loss to the argument have been deferred till it was more distinctly called for. He proceeded to prove that an interference with promissory notes, which were the substitutes for gold, did not involve him in the necessity of meddling with bills of exchange or checks upon bankers — that convertibility was not alone a sufficient guarantee against over issue — that country bankers did not regulate their issues by the foreign exchanges — and that a Government bank was politically dangerous. Thence he unceremoniously leapt to his practical conclusions. " This brought him," he said, " to an explanation of the practical measures which he proposed for the regulation of the matters he had submitted to the consideration of the House."

These measures we have said are just and sagacious; but they are scarcely justified by the speech by which they are introduced. The local banks of issue, for instance, are to be extinguished. Why? We gather from Sir Robert Peel's speech that it is because " they do not control their issues according to the state of the foreign exchanges." And why should they so control them? Because the omission to do so is productive of over issue. And how so? Alas, in this, the very heart and root of the question — the moot point of the whole — Sir Robert leaves us in the dark. The connection between foreign exchanges and English circulation is an interesting and a most important subject; it lay directly between Sir Robert Peel and his conclusion — nay, was the very ground on which that conclusion rested; and, though to a certain extent intricate, is not too abstruse to be handled briefly and conclusively by the first financier of the day. Why, instead of grappling with it, did he spend time in proving what none but a few enthusiasts deny — the inexpediency of a return to paper payments? Equally chary is he of reasons for the proposed separation of the issue and deposit departments of the Bank of England. Those indeed who are familiar with the opinions of the principal mercantile men of the day, or have even mastered the leading pamphlets on those subjects, will be at no loss to divine the principles on which he is proceeding. But this does not meet the wants of the wholly ignorant world, or even we fear of the half-informed House of Commons; and we therefore regret that such an occasion as the present has not drawn from the Premier a fuller and more instructive exposition of those views of currency on which he intends himself, and should persuade his successors, to regulate the circulation of the country."

Unquestionably it is not easy to conceive a more defective or less instructive exposition of views which were destined to have so important a practical application.

Sir Robert Peel had evidently adopted the doctrine of the currency principle in its fullest extent, according to the exposition of it by Mr. Norman and Mr. Loyd; but in his endeavours to explain it to the House, and to show the connection of it with the measure which he was proposing, he failed in a degree which is surprising in a person so gifted, and so generally clear in his statements.

The truth is, that he laboured under the disadvantage of having embraced, without sufficient examination, a theory of the currency which is not accordant with, or explanatory of, the working of the actual system, or calculated to give any distinct insight into the probable effects of the intended change; and more especially of that part of it which relates to the separation of the functions of issue and banking. This measure of separation, for instance, may be the best possible ; but if so, it could not be admitted to be so, for the reasons stated by Sir Robert Peel.

The measures proposed by him, with reference to the regulation of banking, embrace two distinct considerations ; the one is, that which relates to the *quality* of the paper, that is, of the bank notes in circulation, the other relates to the *quantity*.

With respect to the quality of the paper, Sir Robert Peel argues justly against the notion of competition and free trade in banking, so far as relates to the supposition that there would or could be, with due regard to the quality, any benefit or convenience to the public from a competition of banks in the supply of a paper circulation simply on the ground of cheapness. The term cheapness, however, as used by Sir Robert Peel, is hardly appropriate in its application to a supply of bank notes. The only test of their quality, that is, of their value, is their being constantly and instantly convertible, at the will of the holder, into the coin in which they profess to be payable on demand. Not only the value of the notes, as estimated in the coin in which they are payable, but their convenience, is impaired by the slightest hesitation or delay in their conversion into coin when required. The interference of the legislature therefore is perfectly justifiable, to secure the public from the loss and inconvenience attending failure, or even hesitation and delay, on the part of the issuers of notes to fulfil their obligations on demand. And in so far as the proposed measures have that object in view, and are calculated gradually to substitute a more perfect for a less perfect description of paper money, they are entitled to the approbation of the public, which they appear to have received.

Sir Robert Peel, however, is not content with doing away with competition in the issue of promissory notes so far as relates to the quality of the paper, that is, its perfect security and immediate convertibility. He proposes to regulate the quantity of paper money that shall be in the hands of the public, — a matter which stands upon totally different grounds; and he is any thing but happy in his attempts to explain his views on this head, as may be seen in the following passages of his speech : —

The quantity of that article is to be governed by quite other principles than those of competition, because it is definite and fixed, not variable, — fixed in this way, that the amount of paper currency must be determined by the relation it bears to the gold currency. If it exceeds that, then it is in excess. Therefore, all that the country as I think requires is, that it shall have the greatest supply of paper, having its value determined by a corresponding amount of gold, and that that paper shall be issued in quarters entitled to the highest credit. A very different doctrine, however, is supported by those who contend for unlimited competition ; and I beg to call the attention of the House to some of the admissions which they make in the course of their argument in favour of unlimited issue. Those who hold the same opinions as I do contend, that were unlimited competition allowed, although it might be very possible that the issue of notes must ultimately conform, yet that a considerable interval might elapse before that conformity was established, and that the means of establishing it, though certain in their operation, yet would produce great embarrassment and inconvenience before they were entirely successful ; that there is

not that immediate and close sympathy between the issues
of paper and its professed value in gold that there ought to
be ; that the country is not immediately alive to the depreciation that is going on, until ultimately reminded of it by
that silent monitor—gold ; and that by neglecting its early
warnings you force on the Bank the necessity of precipitate
contractions.

Assuming the report (from the *Times*) of this part of
the speech to be correct, I would ask whether it is possible to conceive any thing less clear or more involved
than the view here presented.   The quantity it seems
" is fixed in this way, that the amount of paper currency
must be determined by the relation it bears to the gold
currency.   If it exceeds that, then it is in excess."   No
doubt, if the paper is convertible into gold, it must by
the nature of things, by the very terms of the proposition, be determined in quantity by its relation to
the gold currency.   This is all that I, under the
authority of Adam Smith and Mr. Ricardo, contend
for.   But a conformity of the paper to gold to this
extent is, it seems, not sufficient, because under competition there is not that immediate and close *sympathy* between the issues of paper and its professed
value in gold that there ought to be ; " that the country
is not immediately alive to the depreciation which is
going on until reminded of it by that silent monitor,
gold."

It appears to me that this notion of want of
sympathy between paper and its professed value in
gold, supposing that no doubt exists of its convertibility, is not in point of clearness of conception very un-
like the late Lord Castlereagh's notion that " a pound

*L 5

might be defined to be a sense of value in reference to currency, as compared with commodities."* Because questions analogous to those which are applicable to that definition might be asked, namely, by what rule are you to measure the asserted depreciation of paper, if not by its standard gold? By the prices of commodities; but what commodities? and who is to say whether the circumstances affecting the prices were not sufficient, without supposing the quantity of paper and gold money to be the cause? In short, to the doctrine of depreciation so stated, and often urged by the Birmingham school, no answer but of absolute denial admits of being made.

The error, for such I am intimately persuaded it is, by which a speaker, so eminently clear in general, has been led into this confused statement, is that under the influence of the theory of the currency principle he invests bank notes, without regard to their denomination, with peculiar properties and functions, conferring on them an effect on prices distinct from any which can be produced by other forms of paper credit. And it is not a little curious that in almost the same breath in which the total dissimilarity of bills of exchange and their inapplicability to the same purposes as bank notes is asserted, a threat is held out that if a small bill circulation should be introduced so as to supply the purposes of a bank note circulation within the district of sixty-five miles, the government would be called upon to suppress it.

In the following passage of his speech, Sir Robert Peel objects to unlimited competition in the issue of

---

* Debate on Mr. Vansittart's Resolution, May, 1811.

paper currency, although perfectly and immediately convertible:—

It has been contended by very eminent men that the only security you need take against an excessive issue of paper currency is immediate convertibility. This doctrine, indeed, appears to have the sanction of authorities no less eminent than Adam Smith and Ricardo. They assume that the paper engagement should always be literally fulfilled — that there should be no postponement by means of paper; but they say also, that if you secure practical immediate convertibility, then there will be no immediate apprehension of conversion. If that opinion be not well-founded, it would be no reflection on those eminent men. We are in a constant state of transition, and we are constantly making new discoveries as to the rules which regulate our paper currency. At the same time the House would no doubt be disposed to abandon an opinion sanctioned even by such men as Adam Smith and Ricardo, if from subsequent lights that have been thrown on the subject they should become convinced that they were in error. Now, I shall contend, both upon reason and also upon the admissions of advocates of free competition —and this will be a most difficult and important part of the subject—that convertibility into gold, together with unlimited competition as to issue, does not give sufficient security.

With all deference, I venture to abide by the opinion of Adam Smith and Ricardo as here stated, understanding the sense in which the term convertibility is used, not merely to signify legal liability to conversion, but ability and readiness on the part of the issuers to convert instantly on demand; convertibility not only *de jure* but *de facto* — such perfect convertibility as it is the object of the proposed measure to secure. Subject to this understanding of the term convertibility, I am prepared to maintain that convertibility into gold, together with unlimited competition as to issue, does give sufficient security against an excessive issue of paper currency; by which I mean (and such must be the meaning of Sir Robert Peel, as he expressly excludes bills of exchange and cheques from coming under that designation) bank notes in circulation among the public. The example of banking in America is somewhat inappropriately introduced by Sir Robert Peel, as an example and a warning against allowing the quantity of paper money in the hands of the public to be limited only by its perfect convertibility. The example does not apply, and cannot therefore serve as a warning. Referring to the " individual fortunes ruined, public credit destroyed, and the commerce of the whole of the United States paralysed," he asks, " if immediate convertibility is a check, why has it not operated as such in the United States?" The answer is, that banking in America, as exhibited in Pensylvania and in the other defaulting states, bears not the slightest analogy to banking in this country. Their paper in its issue and in its circulation, including notes of a denomination as low as a quarter of a dollar in value, has partaken of the worst features of a compulsory government paper. The management of the banks, in reckless advances, in many cases to their own directors, on worthless or, unavailable securities, has, under the protection of their defaulting state governments, displayed a combination of fraud and folly unparalleled in the history of banking.

I may much more appropriately adduce, on the contrary, the example of Scotland, the paper currency of which, in point of convertibility, is as nearly as may be perfect, in proof, that under the utmost competition of issue, no excess of circulation of bank notes is, or has been experienced. In point of fact, the circulation in that part of Britain is, notwithstanding the intense competition of banks of issue, reduced to little more than is necessary for mere retail purposes.

A considerable degree of confusion of ideas appears

to be connected with the ambiguous use of the term *issues*. Sir Robert Peel, and the advocates of the currency theory, and, indeed, on this point the mass of the public, seem always, when speaking of *issues*, to associate with the term the idea of bank notes passing into the hands of the public, and remaining out so as to form a part of the circulation; and they use the term *issues* indiscriminately, whether referring to advances by banks of issue in the way of loan or discount, being advances of capital which entail no addition to the amount of notes in circulation, or to the payments of notes over the counter to depositors or others for merely local purposes, and constituting a part of the paper currency of the district. This confusion between advances of capital which do not necessarily entail an addition to the circulation or currency, and the payment of notes over the counter for current purposes is, I apprehend, at the bottom of Sir Robert Peel's dissent from the opinion of Adam Smith and Ricardo, that perfect and immediate convertibility, with unlimited competition of issue, is sufficient security; meaning, of course, against any excess in the amount of bank notes in circulation.

Assuming, as I do, that the quality of the notes, that is, their convertibility is perfect and immediate, there can be no reason for apprehending any danger or inconvenience from the most unlimited competition of banks, as far as regards merely the issue of notes for local purposes; being the only purposes for which they are retained in circulation. The danger of unlimited competition of banks does not apply more to banks of issue, always supposing the notes to be perfect, than to non-issuing banks. The mischief of commercial revulsions from overtrading, whenever traceable to the banks, has been from over advances of capital, on insufficient or inconvertible securities, or both. Banks, whether of issue or not, may, in the competition for business, make advances to persons undeserving of credit, and may discount large amounts of doubtful bills, thus adding to the circulating medium, without adding directly to the amount of the circulation, that is, of notes. Advances so made are, as I have before observed, likely to be recklessly employed, and prices may experience a temporary inflation from credit so unduly extended.* A creation of bills of exchange and deposits must be the certain consequence: and the circulation of bills of exchange while the banks are in credit, might sustain the extended transactions for

---

* I would here take the opportunity of observing that my argument in the preceding pages has been directed to the purpose of pointing out the error, as I believe it to be, of the currency theory in ascribing to the discrepancy between the fluctuations of bank notes and bullion, evils, exclusive of the danger of inconvertibility of the paper, and insolvency of the issuing banks. I have, therefore, guarded myself in my reference to the distinctive character of issuing and non-issuing banks, in their influence on the circulation, and on prices, by the assumption that the advances were made on sufficient securities. It is accordingly with no little surprise that I find, in a pamphlet recently published by Sir William Clay, the following passage: " It is to me, indeed, matter of great surprise that, by Mr. Tooke especially, the power of banks of issue to add to the amount of the circulating medium should be denied. To those who will only admit that notes should be considered as money, the evidence which clearly proves the occasional difficulty of forcing them into, or retaining them in, circulation, might be embarrassing, but to Mr. Tooke, who contends, and justly, that deposits are equally to be considered as money, I cannot understand how the proposition that the power of issuing notes does confer on banks a direct and most effective means of adding to the circulating medium of the country can be denied." Now, I beg leave most emphatically to deny that I ever denied the power of banks of issue to add to the circulating medium, including in that term deposits and bills of exchange. I merely denied that banks of issue had that power (the local circulation being supposed to be full) in a greater degree than non-issuing banks. It never entered into my head to imagine, much less to state distinctly, that banks, whether issuing or non-issuing, had not the power of adding by bills of exchange and deposits to the circulating medium. Indeed, nobody can have been more alive than I have been to the fact, and I have before stated it, that the banks, both issuing and non-issuing, were instrumental by an undue extension of credit in 1835, 1836, to an excessive circulation of bills of exchange. This mistake materially affects the greater part of the arguments urged in opposition to my views in Sir William Clay's pamphlet.

some time, without the intervention of bank notes. The recoil of the speculation and overtrading would, in most cases, not be caused in the first instance by a want of bank notes, but by a want of demand from a view to the supply and consumption. The speculators, and perhaps the bankers, might then fail. And all this without any competition in the issue of n.tes. Now, there is no provision in the proposed measures to prevent such over advances by banks, whether joint-stock or not.

Without dwelling on the incongruity and inconclusiveness of the reasoning against the competition of banks of issue under a system of actual, perfect, and immediate convertibility, there remains to notice the scheme for the regulation of the Bank of England upon the renewal of the charter. This is to consist in a separation of the business of the establishment into two departments, the one of Issue, and the other of Banking, to be kept as distinct in the management except in being under the same roof and the same management, as if they were two entirely separate establishments. For the precise grounds of this separation, we may search in vain through the speech of Sir R. Peel. On the face of the scheme, all that is proposed by it might be effected by mere bookkeeping, or still more simply by the practice of prudent, well-conducted banks, of keeping such a reserve as according to all human means of calculation, from experience and observation, would enable them to meet all their liabilities.

The reason, although not distinctly stated as the ground for the proposed measure, may be collected from the concluding part of Sir Robert Peel's speech, in which, with not a little of declamation and exaggeration, he descants on the magnitude of the evils arising out of the present system, which he has in view to remedy. Among the evils so dwelt upon, in addition to the failures of banks, and the losses and suffering which they have inflicted on a large part of the community, and of which his measures for the regulation of the issues of private and joint stock banks are intended to prevent the recurrence; he refers to the fluctuations of the currency, since 1819 " so dangerous to all commercial enterprise, and defeating all calculations upon which commercial enterprise could rest," and he speaks of " the danger arising from the Bank of England having recourse to foreign establishments."

It is to be hence presumed, that of the two objects in view by this measure, the one is to have the bank issues regulated by the foreign exchanges with a view to prevent fluctuation; the other to avert the danger of a suspension of cash payments.

To speak of the last first, I should say that if the measure of separation were calculated to insure the convertibility under any conceivable circumstances of a suspension of cash payments, this consideration alone would reconcile me to the measure, whatever might be the inconvenience of the working of it which I might anticipate. But I doubt the greater security against suspension, held out by this measure.

If the emergency should occur, such as in 1797 or in 1825, it would depend entirely upon the character of the ministry of the day whether they would not authorise the issuing department to assist the banking department to its own exhaustion. The obstacle, by the separation, to an order in council for restriction, if applied for by the directors, and coming within the views of policy of a ministry backed by a strong majority in parliament, would be absolutely nothing. And nothing better or more secure, probably much less so, would be a government bank of issue. The first disastrous turn of an expensive war, combined with a state of trade determining an efflux of the metals. would be the occasion of suspension. I should much sooner rely for security against such a calamity, on the prudence of a set of directors, having no sinister interest, and enlightened by the experience of the effects of former mismanagement.

I leave altogether out of the question the consideration of profit to the state, which is utterly insignificant, if there were not only this nominal separation, but a national establishment for the issue of a government paper. We are now only discussing how far the separation is likely, besides security against suspension, to remedy the evils so eloquently referred to by Sir Robert Peel, of the fluctuations of the currency so dangerous to all commercial enterprise.

I do not believe that it will provide any such remedy. Let us see what the operation of it is likely to be.

Nothing is yet known as to the exact form in which the accounts of the Bank under the new arrangement are to be laid before the public. But the statements periodically given under the existing system furnish data for judging of the position at starting (supposing no material alteration since the last Gazette return of 20th April) of the banking department, which, inasmuch as the issuing department is to be perfectly passive, is the only one the working of which will exercise any influence on the money market, in other words, on the rate of interest and the state of credit. By the last quarterly return, the amount of the circulation (notes in the hands of the public) was 21,427,000*l.*, of deposits 13,615,000*l.*, and of bullion 16,015,000*l.* In the issuing department, the whole of the amount of notes beyond the 14,000,000*l.* of fixed securities to be held by it, must be considered as issued against bullion. Consequently, of the above amount of 16,015,000*l.*, there will belong to the issuing department, 7,427,000*l.*

The remainder, 8,588,000*l.*, will belong to the banking department; but as notes will be found more convenient for it to hold than bullion, the probability is, that the reserve of the banking department will be held in notes. The banking department will then hold 8,588,000*l.* as a reserve, in notes or bullion at its option, against 13,615,000*l.* of deposits, which will then apparently be its only liabilities.*

There being just now so unprecedented an amount of bullion in the coffers of the Bank, subject to the separation here described, not the slightest sensible effect is likely to be produced by the separation at this time, and so far it has a fair chance in its trial, there being no present inconvenience from the experiment. The impression under which this separation has been made is, that the circulation will by this means be regulated by the exchanges; but in what sense? Is it meant according to the exposition (see p. 4. *antè*) that the circulation is to vary with the export and import of bullion ?

Circulation, as hitherto defined in the examinations by the Banking Committee, and in the publications of the advocates of the currency theory, was distinctly understood to be the amount of bank notes in the hands of the public.

Taking the circulation in this sense, if a demand were suddenly to arise for gold for export, it probably would fall on the banking department, let us say wholly, to the extent of five millions. The banking department would, having so large a reserve, meet this demand by taking the five millions of bank notes to the circulating department, in exchange for gold.

---

* It is immaterial in this view to state the amount of securities which will figure in the banking department. In the return of the 20th of April, they stood at 22,150,000*l.*, from which would be to be deducted the 3,000,000*l.* of exchequer bills allotted to the issuing department.

The circulating department would then have five millions less of bullion, and the banking department five millions less in bank notes, retaining still what might be considered as a sufficient reserve. But the amount of bank notes in the hands of the public would be exactly the same as it had been. Can it then be said that the effect of this operation would be that of contracting the circulation, and so improving the exchanges. The exchanges would be favourably affected by the export of so much gold; but could not by possibility be influenced by any increased value of our currency, supposed to be the effect of a diminished amount of it.

In what respect would the operation of a demand for five millions of gold, so satisfied by this double process, be different in any conceivable point of view, from the operation of a similar demand under the existing system? One should suppose that this view ought to serve as a corrective of the currency theory of the effects of an efflux and influx of bullion; and it is to be observed that neither during the influx of the last five millions imported was there the slightest effect observable on the amount of the circulation.

As long as the stock of bullion is large in the banking department, the working of the new system will be precisely the same as the old. So much attention has been drawn to the state of the Bank as connected with the money market and commercial affairs generally, that an export of five millions would give rise to all sorts of opinions, as many wrong as right. But I am supposing the operation divested of the influence of opinion. A possible process, however, leading to this operation, might have some curious effects.

Suppose the Bank no longer under the necessity which it may have felt before, of considering the state of feeling of the money dealing and mercantile interests, were with a view of not holding so unreasonably large a reserve, to make a forcible operation by reducing the rate of their periodical advances to 1 per cent., and their rate of discount to 1½ per cent. This would inevitably have the effect of forcing a large amount of capital out of the country, from absolute despair of employment within it. It would go into the foreign dividend paying funds, such as the French, Dutch, Prussian, and Danish stocks, and into the foreign railway shares, and other investments abroad. This under the existing system would be described as the Bank forcing out its *issues* of paper, although the bank notes would only pass from one department to the other. But after the operation had been completed, and the effect felt in the export of five millions of bullion, leaving three millions and a half as the reserve of the banking department, the operation of any further demand for gold, if only to the extent of one and a half to two millions, would have a very sensible operation on the money market. The necessity for adopting precautionary measures, in calling in or selling securities, would be urgent, so that the money dealers and others might, having relied upon continued abundance of money, be exposed to be taken by surprise and called upon by their depositors, payable on demand, for sums which might oblige them in their turn to call in their advances.

The Bank would be applied to for discount, but it might refuse altogether or raise the rate very high. Under these circumstances then, there would be a severe pressure on the money market, and a rise in the rate of interest not improbably much beyond 5 per cent.

Take another case; supposing the Bank to have a fair amount of treasure compared with its liabilities, namely, three to three and a half millions, and, as before, a demand for gold to the extent of one and a half to two millions. Trade might be increasing, circumstances favourable to speculation, and overtrading might arise. Now, speculations and overtrading in their origin and during a considerable period of their progress, if favoured by circumstances, proceed in most cases on simple credit. Bills are some time after taken, and not unfrequently renewed to wait the event of markets. If these turn out to be unfavourable, the acceptors are called upon to pay at maturity; they apply for discount, but this is difficult; the doors of the Bank are shut and the money dealers impracticable. Supposing this to occur at a time of a great failure of the crops, entailing a considerable demand for foreign corn, it is quite within moderate probability that the market rate of interest and discount might rise to 15 or 20 per cent. And all this while the circulating department might have at least six or eight millions of gold in its coffers.

I might by further illustrations show to what considerable fluctuation in the rate of interest this rigid adherence to the separation, with a full stock of gold in the issuing department, would subject the trading and manufacturing classes. But enough has here been stated fully to justify the opinion expressed at the close of the series of conclusions at page 124.

That a total separation of the business of issue from that of banking is calculated to produce greater and more abrupt transitions in the rate of interest and the state of credit, than the present system of union of the departments.

THE END.